NORTH KOREAN ONSLAUGHT

UN STAND AT THE PUSAN PERIMETER AUGUST–SEPTEMBER 1950

GERRY VAN TONDER

Pen & Sword
MILITARY

To my wife Tracey

A woman flees P'ohang, October 1950. (Photo US Navy)

First published in Great Britain in 2018 by
PEN AND SWORD MILITARY
an imprint of
Pen and Sword Books Ltd
47 Church Street
Barnsley
South Yorkshire S70 2AS

Copyright © Gerry van Tonder, 2018

ISBN 978 1 52672 833 3

Typeset by Aura Technology and Software Services, India
Maps, drawings and militaria in the colour section by Colonel Dudley Wall
Printed and bound by CPI Group (UK) Ltd, Croydon CR0 4YY

Pen & Sword Books Ltd incorporates the imprints of Pen & Sword
Archaeology, Atlas, Aviation, Battleground, Discovery, Family History, History, Maritime, Military,
Naval, Politics, Railways, Select, Social History, Transport, True Crime, Claymore Press, Frontline
Books, Leo Cooper, Praetorian Press, Remember When, Seaforth Publishing and Wharncliffe.

For a complete list of Pen and Sword titles please contact
Pen and Sword Books Limited
47 Church Street, Barnsley, South Yorkshire, S70 2AS, England
email: enquiries@pen-and-sword.co.uk
website: www.pen-and-sword.co.uk

CONTENTS

GLOSSARY

APC	armour-piercing capped
DPRK	Democratic People's Republic of Korea (North Korea)
EUSAK	Eighth United States Army in Korea
FAB	field artillery battalion
FEAF	Far East Air Force (US)
HE	high explosive
HVAP	high-velocity armour-piercing
JOC	Joint Operations Center
KATUSA	Korean Augmentation to the US Army
KMAG	Korea Military Advisory Group (US)
KPA	Korean People's Army (North Korean)
MLR	main line of resistance
MSR	main supply route
NSC	National Security Council
PRC	People's Republic of China
RCT	Regimental Combat Team
ROK	Republic of Korea (South Korea)
ROKA	Republic of Korea Army (South Korean)
TACP	Tactical Air Control Party
UN	United Nations
UNC	United Nations Command
UNTCOK	United Nations Temporary Commission on Korea
USAFIK	US Army Forces in Korea

TIMELINE

1894–95
Japan and China resort to conflict to determine ownership of Korea. China is defeated.

1904
The Russo-Japanese War breaks out, as the two competing imperial powers in the region fight over southern Manchuria and Korea.

1905
After a conclusive Japanese naval victory at the battle of Tsushima in May 1905, in which two-thirds of the Russian fleet are destroyed, Japanese troops take Seoul, shooting Korean Prime Minister Han Kyu-sŏl who refuses to relegate power to Japan. Japan affords Korea protectorate status.

1910
Japan formally annexes Korea. Emperor Sunjong of the Yi dynasty relinquishes his authority to Japan.

1919
Korean activists, calling themselves the 1st March, or Samil, Movement, read out the Korean declaration of independence in Seoul, sparking the first major resistance to the Japanese occupation.

1925
18 April: The Communist Party of Korea, led by Kim Yŏng-bom and Pak Hŏn-yŏng, is secretly formed in Seoul.

1940
Amphibious Japanese forces move into Indochina.

1941
7 December: Japan attacks Pearl Harbor.

1945
4–11 February: At Yalta, the western Allies and the Soviet Union agree to a post-war trusteeship of Korea.

15 August: Japan surrenders.

US President Truman signs the instrument allowing for the temporary divide of the Korean peninsula at the 38th Parallel: Soviet forces to the north and American forces to the south.

The Allies agree to the setting up of a joint US–Soviet commission to facilitate a process that will culminate in Korean independence.

1946
Kim Il-sung, who had spent the latter half of the war training with Soviet troops, is appointed the head of a Marxist-Leninist provisional government in the Soviet zone.

1947
A second US–Soviet meeting to discuss Korea's future also ends in deadlock.

September: The US takes the Korean question to the United Nations; the UN accepts a US-endorsed plan for global elections in Korea to vote for a single government.

1948
North Korea refuses to allow the United Nations Temporary Commission on Korea (UNTCOK) across the 'border'.

UNTCOK declares that elections should go ahead in all areas that allowed the commission access.

The Korean People's Army (KPA) in North Korea is formalized.

American joint chiefs of staff urge the withdrawal of US forces from Korea.

April: US President Truman accepts the National Security Council's (NSC) paper No. 8 as the basis for America's foreign policy on Korea: to assist with military training and the Korean economy only, and not with its defence.

Elections are held, but only in South Korea. Syngman Rhee is elected the first president of South Korea and the Republic of Korea (ROK) is established.

Separate elections in North Korea result in the formation of the Supreme People's Assembly. The Democratic People's Republic of Korea (DPRK) is proclaimed, with Kim Il-sung as the first North Korean leader.

Moscow withdraws its troops from North Korea.

The UN declares that the ROK is the only legitimate Korean government.

1949

The last US combat forces leave South Korea.

The US Korea Military Advisory Group (KMAG) commences its work.

Mao Zedong proclaims the communist People's Republic of China (PRC).

1950

March: After investigating rumours of an impending North Korean invasion of the south, US military intelligence find that it is not imminent.

June: The DPRK makes public its plans for a unified Korea.

25 June: Massed North Korean troops, armour and artillery cross the 38th Parallel invading South Korea.; United Nations Security Council Resolution 82 is adopted demanding that North Korea immediately ceases its invasion of South Korea and withdraws its troops.

27 June: US Far East Air Force (FEAF) is deployed to provide air cover for the evacuation from Seoul to the port of Inch'ŏn; the UN comes out against the invasion, calling it a breach of peace; US Seventh Fleet moves into station in the Formosa Straits.

28 June: Korean People's Army (KPA) takes Seoul.

29 June: US commences bombing of selected targets in the DPRK.

30 June: US President Truman consents to the deployment of ground troops in Korea and orders a mobilization of reserves.

1 July: Elements of the US 24th Infantry Division—Task Force Smith—arrive in Korea.

5 July: Task Force Smith sustains heavy losses as it withdraws from Osan.

7 July: United Nations Security Council Resolution 84 is adopted, calling on UN members to assist South Korea with whatever may be necessary to repel the North Korean invasion.

8 July: Pursuant to a UN request for the US to assume control of UN peace efforts in Korea, Truman appoints General Douglas MacArthur to head United Nations Command (UNC) forces.

10 July: US 25th Infantry Division starts arriving in Korea from Japan.

12 July: Lieutenant General Walton H. Walker is placed in command of UNC ground troops.

18 July: US 1st Cavalry Division starts arriving in Korea.

20 July: KPA takes Taejŏn as the US 24th and 25th infantry divisions counterattack at Okch'ŏn to stall the KPA while defences are strengthened along the Naktong River.

29 July: The first of the US 2nd Infantry Division starts arriving in Korea.

1 August: Yakov Malik, Soviet delegate to the UN, takes over as president of the UN Security Council.

2 August: US 1st Provisional Marine Brigade arrives in Korea; US I Corps is mobilized at Fort Bragg in readiness for deployment to Korea.

4 August: UNC forces dig in along the Naktong River, in what becomes known as the Pusan Perimeter.

4 August: First battle of Naktong Bulge commences.

7 August: In the first UN counterattack of the war, a combined US army and Marines force—Task Force Kean—attacks the Korean People's Army (KPA) 6th Division at Chinju.

9 August: A KPA division attempts to strike south along the east coast.

15 August: US Eighth Army begins recruiting South Koreans, known as Korean Augmentation to the US Army (KATUSA).

27 August: KPA launches a fresh wave of well-coordinated attacks on the perimeter.

31 August: Second battle of Naktong Bulge commences.

6 September: Republic of Korea Army (ROKA) forces are pushed out of P'ohang by the North Koreans.

10 September: KPA forces push US troops back to within fifteen miles of Taegu.

12 September: North Korean assault on the Pusan Perimeter stalls.

15 September: US X Corps lands at Inch'ŏn on the west coast, to the rear of the North Koreans.

16 September: US Eighth Army commences its breakout.

23 September: North Korean forces begin a general withdrawal from the Pusan Perimeter front.

INTRODUCTION

In the first volume in this series by the author on the Korean War, *North Korea Invades the South*, an account is given of North Korean ground forces, armour and artillery crossing the 38th Parallel on 25 June 1950, and how, in blitzkrieg style, they rolled back US and South Korean forces down the Korean peninsula.

Exploiting the element of surprise, KPA forces, led by tanks, had quickly over-run Ongjin in the west, and with more than 50 tanks spearheading a column of 8–10,000 troops, struck down the historical Poch'ŏn–Ŭijŏngbu corridor to the South Korean capital, Seoul. US Fifth Air Force and naval resources in Japan were placed on standby for the evacuation of American civilians. In Japan, US Far East Command, in the absence of a contingency to systematically deal with the unexpected crisis in Korea, was frantically busy preparing and disseminating orders to facilitate optimum deployment.

General George Stratemeyer arrived back at the US Haneda Army Air Base (today Tokyo International) to resume control of the US Far East Air Force (FEAF). The strategic bombing of selected targets in North Korea commenced as US Twentieth Air Force Boeing B-29 Superfortress heavy bombers raided the North Korean air station at Wonsan.

Early in July, North Korean infantry and armour crossed the Han River, before straddling the main arterial route south of Seoul as the Korean People's Army's (KPA's) 2nd, 3rd and 6th divisions pushed down the western Suwŏn–Ch'ŏnan–Taejŏn axis. Rolling back the US Eighth Army's 24th Division, commanded by Major General William F. Dean, the unstoppable North Koreans enveloped Suwŏn.

At the same time, six C-54 transports ferried the eponymous Task Force Smith from Japan to Pusan, from where the unit was transported by train north to the South Korean town of Taejon, arriving in the South Korean town the following morning. The force comprised half of battalion headquarters company, half of the signals platoon, and below-strength B and C rifle companies: 406 officers and men. Lieutenant Colonel Charles B. Smith, commanding officer, 1st Battalion, 21st Regiment, 24th Infantry Division, was tasked with executing a delaying action pending the arrival of the US 24th and 25th divisions. Woefully underequipped, Smith's position near Suwŏn stood little chance against the Soviet-made North Korean T-34/85 tanks from the 107th Tank Regiment, KPA 105th Armoured Division at the head of the North Korean column. In the ensuing rout, the American task force ceased to be a recognizable combat unit. American troops abandoned their arms and equipment, 'bomb-shelling' into the countryside.

In the author's words in *North Korea Invades the South: Across the 38th Parallel, June 1950*:

The wisdom of America's precipitate entry in the war, largely fuelled by an impulsive MacArthur, will always come under critical scrutiny. To send a tiny, disjointed, ill-prepared and poorly equipped 'task force' to dam the Red tsunami from above the 38th Parallel, was a totally ill-conceived and naïve blunder by the decision-makers in both Tokyo and Washington. For Smith and his gallant party of mainly inexperienced young men, it was a suicide mission, which, at best, merely slowed the North Korean advance by seven hours ... Kim Il-sung's army continued on its southward blitzkrieg, ploughing through the 34th Regiment's 'blocking position' at P'yŏngt'aek on 6 July.

Lieutenant Colonel Harold 'Red' Ayres, commander of the 1st Battalion, US 34th Infantry Regiment (1/34th), suffered the same fate as Task Force Smith, as Major General Lee Kwon Mu's KPA 4th Infantry Division pulverized the US position, sending the Americans reeling southward in complete disarray.

On 7 July, the United Nations (UN) Security Council adopted Resolution 84, calling on member states to assist with whatever means at their disposal to clear the south of the North Korean invaders. The sometimes controversial Second World War US army veteran and icon, General Douglas MacArthur, was quickly appointed commander of United Nations Command (UNC) forces, tasked with the implementation of the UN resolution. A few days earlier, the US 24th Division's commander, Major General William F. Dean, had assumed command of the US Army Forces in Korea (USAFIK). The 51-year-old general set up his headquarters, together with that of his division, at Taejŏn.

Relentlessly, North Korean forces pushed southward. On 8 July, the KPA 16th and 18th infantry regiments, 4th Division, with T-34/85 tanks in support, pushed the US 34th Regiment out of Ch'ŏnan.

On 13 July, the US Eighth Army established its headquarters in South Korea, commanded by Lieutenant General Walton 'Johnnie Walker' Walker. A veteran of both world wars, and former XX Corps commander in General George S. Patton's US Third Army in the Northwest Europe campaign of the Second World War, the short, stocky Texan was twice awarded the Distinguished Service Cross for extraordinary heroism, the Distinguished Service Medal for distinguished or meritorious Service twice, the Silver Star for gallantry on three occasions, the Legion of Merit for exceptional meritorious conduct, the Distinguished Flying Cross for heroism in an aerial flight twice, the Bronze Star for heroic or meritorious achievement or service, and on 12 occasions, the Air Medal for meritorious achievement while participating in aerial flight.

Soviet-made T-34-85 medium tank. (Photo Vitaly V. Kuzmin)

A leader with such a pedigree in combat was needed to restore morale and turn the humiliating situation around.

The South Korean army was close to total implosion, and the closest American reinforcements would have to come from occupied Japan, where the US 25th Infantry and 1st Cavalry divisions were being mobilized. From 10 July, the US 25th Division started arriving in South Korea, followed on the 18th by the US 1st Cavalry which landed at P'ohang on the east coast.

Some 5,500 troops of Major General Dean's battered US 24th Division, in a defensive line on the Kŭm River between KPA-held Ch'ŏnan and Taejŏn, were soon overwhelmed as elements of the 16th Regiment, KPA 4th Division, started crossing the Kŭm on the US 34th's left flank.

A week later, Lieutenant General Walker arrived on a fleeting visit to tell Major General William Frishe Dean to hold Taejŏn with his US 24th Division for at least two more days to allow him to deploy the US 1st Cavalry, fresh from Japan, on the road to the south. About 4,000 Americans had entered the battle to prevent Taejŏn from becoming another North Korean victim, but, on 21 July, Taejŏn also fell. More than 1,100 had become casualties, but the greatest—and most embarrassing—loss, was that of divisional commander General Dean, who had become separated from his men and captured by the North Koreans. Major General Church would assume command, with Dean listed as missing in action.

Low morale in the US 24th Regiment had now taken on pandemic proportions, despite the deployment into the theatre of American troop reinforcements from Japan. So great was the threat of the regiment's demeanour collapsing the American line, that military roadblocks were established to the south to stem the flow of GI deserters from the front.

To the east, elements of the South Korean army had been falling back in the face of an overpowering onslaught by the KPA 15th Division. Situated in the centre of South Korea, the town of Sangju sits on the mountain-road junction just south of the Mun'gyŏng plateau. The dividing watershed between the Han and Naktong rivers, which provided a commanding vista of the Naktong valley, made Sangju a desirable strategic objective.

Recognizing the imminent danger of allowing the North Koreans to enter the Naktong River valley, General Walker immediately ordered Major General William B. Kean's 13,000-strong US 25th Division to take over the responsibility of securing the front to the north of Sangju from the crumbling South Korean ground forces. Over the next few days, however, the American–South Korean line protecting the two access routes into Sangju also began faltering.

By 27 July, the KPA had taken the Mun'gyŏng divide and were penetrating the upper reaches of the Naktong valley near Hamch'ang. Simultaneously, the inexperienced young troops of the KPA 15th Division attacked Sangju, while to the west KPA units were advancing along the secondary road from the mountains. Here too, there were cases of American troops discarding their weapons and fleeing in panic and disarray.

In a rolling series of engagements, the US 24th Infantry Regiment—the only force remaining to hold Sangju—supported by batteries from three field artillery battalions (FABS), was slowly retiring back along the western route to Sangju, pushed by elements of the KPA 15th Division. Casualties were mounting on both sides, while the Americans' resupply became increasingly tenuous. A cycle of fighting the North Koreans by day then falling back under cover of darkness evolved.

At last light on 29 July, all that was remaining on the front line at night, were commander of the US 24th Regiment, Colonel Horton V. White, a combat engineer company and a battery of field artillery. Frantically defending their position, that night the artillery battery fired in excess of 3,000 rounds into the darkness to keep the North Koreans at a comfortable distance.

That same day, Walker ordered Colonel John H. 'Iron Mike' Michaelis to withdraw his 27th Regiment to take up a new position just to the east of Kimch'ŏn. Later that same day, Eighth Army Headquarters issued fresh orders for Michaelis to move farther southeast to Waegwan on the Naktong River, close to Taegu.

The US 1st Cavalry Division, initially preparing to fill the gap in the front line left by the withdrawal of the 27th, was then threatened by the KPA 3rd Division skirting their left flank and taking Kimch'ŏn, and, in doing so, cutting off Gay's vital supply line to Pusan.

Eventually, during the night of 31 July, the 24th Infantry Regiment withdrew through Sangju, leaving the North Korean 15th Division to set up a new defensive line at Sangju the next day. The US 25th Infantry Division was moved to deal with a growing attack on Masan to the south.

On 31 July, the US 1st Cavalry was moved to the Naktong River. By executing what may, in hindsight, be regarded as rearguard actions, the retiring US 1st Cavalry, and US 24th and 25th divisions had secured the UNC forces sufficient time to establish the defensive Pusan Perimeter.

On 1 August, General Walker at US Eighth Army HQ directed all United Nations Command ground forces in Korea to commence a planned withdrawal to the east of the Naktong River. The main defensive positions of the Pusan Perimeter would then be established. The objective would be to stall the KPA's southerly advance while the UNC built up its forces in readiness for a counteroffensive.

The US 25th Infantry Division was deployed to the extreme southern point of Walker's left flank at Masan, while the US24th Infantry Division dug in at Kŏch'ang, also on the left flank. The US 1st Cavalry Division retired to Waegwan to the northwest of Taegu. As they withdrew, the Americans destroyed all bridges over the Naktong River.

Key to the success of the UNC defensive plan was to hold Pusan at all costs. The port received vital war matériel and reinforcements from both occupied Japan and the United States, while the city possessed airfields where combat and cargo aircraft were arriving with more supplies. A truck convoy system, resembling the famed Red Ball Express of the Second World War that supplied Allied forces moving quickly through Europe after breaking out from the D-Day beaches in Normandy, was introduced to get supplies from Pusan to the front lines.

The North Korean forces had four possible routes of ingression into the perimeter:

1. to the south via the city of Masan, at the confluence of the Nam and Naktong rivers;
2. through the Naktong Bulge on the UNC's left flank, and on to the railway lines at Miryang;
3. into Taegu, a major road and rail hub, and Eighth Army HQ to the north;
4. along the eastern corridor from P'ohang-dong and through Kyongju.

CAN AMERICANS HOLD ON TO KOREA?

It's Men—Not Machines—That Are Needed
By A Military Correspondent

The next five or six days will be vital in Korea. The position in a nutshell is this. At present we have more planes, tanks and big guns than we can effectively handle. We haven't got a fraction of the infantry we need. And Korea is definitely infantry country.

The reason for the continual retreat of the American land forces over the past two weeks has been that their great weight armour has only been able to operate on the few, narrow, mostly unmetalled, roads. All the hills around them have been the unchallenged playground of the North Korean infantry. The infantry can't be bulldozed out of the hills. They've got to be winkled out. And only infantry can do it.

So the immediate fate of Korea depends on how soon and in what numbers we can get men—not machines—into the field of action. The men are on the way. The nearest reinforcements at the moment are the U.S. 1st Marine Division and the U.S. 2nd Infantry Division. They're about five days' sailing time away. The only port at which they could be put ashore and organized for a forward thrust is Pusan.

General MacArthur's tactics are to make a slow withdrawal to this vital bridgehead. The withdrawal will go on, if necessary, until the whole strength of his armour is drawn around a small perimeter to form a siegewall, behind which the lifesaving infantry can land. The terrain is suitable for this kind of action. With any luck at all, evacuation should not be necessary.

North Korea has nine full divisions in attack, with probably as many in reserve. It's unlikely U.N. Forces will attempt a large-scale offensive until they can at least equal the North Koreans in manpower. There is one possible snag. Strong forces of Manchurian troops are known to be massed in the north. They have not yet been ordered forward, for political reasons. If they were suddenly rushed in, the whole picture might be altered.

The next five or six days, and the speed with which more land forces can be mustered after that, is the vital factor.

Sunday Post, Sunday, 30 July 1950

Wounded in combat. An American infantryman of the segregated 24th Regiment, US 25th Infantry Division. (Photo US Army)

In their major August 1950 offensive, the North Koreans simultaneously struck at all four entry points into the perimeter. The defence of the Pusan Perimeter, therefore, comprised a series of large-scale battles punctuated by numerous smaller engagements, and characterized by Walker's constant troop movements to confront widespread KPA incursions.

1. DEFENCE OF MASAN

Merged with the contiguous cities of Changwon and Jinhae in 2010 to form Unified Ch'angwŏn City, the port city of Masan lies 35 miles west of South Korea's second-largest city, Busan, known at the time of the Korean War as Pusan.

From 5 August to 19 September 1950, combined American and South Korean forces under the United Nations Command faced concerted attacks by the Korean People's Army 6th and 7th divisions to breach the southern extremity of the Pusan Perimeter's left flank in the vicinity of Masan.

By 31 July, Walker had pulled back all elements of his US Eighth Army south and east of the Naktong River, with the exception of those forces tasked with holding the KPA west of Chinju and Masan. Here, the 20,000-strong Task Force Kean faced KPA forces numbering some 20,000. Commanded by Major General William B. Kean, the UNC task force comprised the US 25th Infantry Division (24th, 27th and 35th infantry regiments), the US 5th Regimental Combat Team (RCT), the US 1st Marine Brigade and elements of the South Korea National Police.

A 1918 graduate of West Point, the 53-year-old Kean, by the end of the Second World War and with the rank of brigadier general, held the position of chief of staff of the US First Army. In September 1948, the highly regarded and respected general was given command of the US 25th Infantry Division in occupied Japan.

The North Korean forces opposite Kean in the sector comprised the KPA 6th and 7th infantry divisions. Commanded by General Pang Ho San, the KPA 6th Infantry Division (13th, 14th and 15th infantry regiments, and the 6th Artillery Regiment) actively participated in the initial invasion of the south on 25 June. Notwithstanding heavy losses at Inch'ŏn, the division had struck down the peninsula's west coast virtually unhindered. The combat-untried KPA 12th Infantry Division (30th, 31st and 32nd infantry regiments), under General Paek Nak Chil, had initially been deployed to the rear of the KPA 6th Division to protect strategic ports.

In the first major UNC offensive since the North Koreans crossed the 38th Parallel, Walker was desirous of taking the war to the North Koreans, seen by many as a much-needed morale-boosting expedition. Task Force Kean would be given the responsibility of executing the offensive.

On 1 August, the first elements of the newly activated 1st Provisional Marine Brigade—designated Task Group 53.7—started to arrive at Pusan by sea from San Diego. Essentially a bolstered combat-ready 5th Marine Regiment (5th Marines), the 6,600-strong brigade included artillery of the 1st Battalion, 11th Marine Regiment (105mm howitzers), the 1st Tank Battalion (new M26 Pershing tanks), Marine Aircraft

Group 33 (F4U Corsairs), an engineer battalion and various support echelons. Pacific theatre veteran Brigadier General Edward A. 'Eddie' Craig was given command of the brigade, with Lieutenant Colonel Raymond Murray commanding the 5th Marines. Late on the night of 2 August, Craig received his orders from Eighth Army HQ to move his ground elements west to the Ch'angwŏn area, just to the rear of the US 25th Division.

At the same time, at Kobe in Japan, Marine fighter squadron VMF-214 'Black Sheep', Marine Air Group 33, was preparing to embark on the USS *Sicily* (CVE-118) for operations in Korean waters. After two days of field carrier training at Itami Air Force Base, Japan, on 3 August the squadron's twenty-four gull-winged Chance Vought F4U Corsairs flew out to the *Sicily* which had been cruising in the Tsushima Straits.

Later that same afternoon, eight Corsairs carried out the first sortie against KPA forces in the vicinity of the city of Chinju (also Jinju), about 30 miles to the west of Masan. During the month of August, the squadron logged over 1,700 combat hours, destroying 12 T-34 type tanks, 40 trucks, three anti-aircraft and four anti-tank weapons, five artillery pieces, 15 mortars and eleven machine guns. An estimated 1,250 casualties were inflicted on the KPA.

A Vought F4U-4B Corsair of Marine Fighter Squadron VMF-214 being readied for launching from the escort carrier USS *Sicily* (CVE-118), August 1950. (Photo US Navy)

CG FMFPAC 1tr 120; jbc P20–1 23 Aug 50
Re: Performance of Duty

1. The Commanding General, Fleet Marine Force, Pacific, extends his heartiest congratulations to the officers and men of the Forward Echelon 1st Marine Air Wing for their outstanding performance of duty during the past three weeks in combat operations against the enemy of Korea.
2. The splendid close air support, both carrier and shore based which you have rendered to your comrades in the ground forces of the 1st Provisional Marine Brigade (Reinforced), as well as to other elements of the 8th Army, has not only caused the enemy heavy casualties but is responsible for saving many lives of your fellow Marines and Soldiers on the ground.
3. I assure you that I express the sentiment of the whole Marine Corps as well as that of the American Public when I say "Well Done", we are all proud of you.

/s/ Lemuel C. Shepherd, Jr. LtGen, USMC.
(Korean War Project Record, VMF-214, Historical Diary, July–December 1950)

By early August 1950, feasibility assessments by the US Eighth Army's G-3 planning section, combined with the arrival of reinforcements and army intelligence, persuaded General Walker, albeit reluctantly, to endorse his general staff's plans for the UNC's first counterattack of the conflict. The attack would be conducted in the direction of Chinju more than 40 miles by road directly west of the port city of Masan, along a 20-mile-wide corridor. The offensive would be carried out by the US 25th Infantry Division, and named for the division's commander, Major General William B. Kean: Task Force Kean. Kean's set objective was to use his assault on Chinju to lure further KPA units southward, away from the beleaguered Taegu to the north.

Although the division was without its 27th Infantry Regiment and the 8th Field Artillery Battalion, numbers were supplemented by the attachment of the newly arrived 5th Regimental Combat Team and the 1st Provisional Marine Brigade. Included were the 89th and 1st Marine medium tank battalions, respectively equipped with M4A3 Sherman and M26 Pershing tanks.

From the evening of 5 August and through the following day, the Fifth Air Force was tasked with isolating the intended battlefield, preventing KPA reinforcements from entering the corridor.

A Marine M26 Pershing tank grinds up high ground along the Naktong River, 1950. (Photo Sergeant Frank Kerr)

Kean planned to split his force into three to secure the strategic Chinju Pass and the line of the Nam River. To the north, the 35th 'Cacti' Infantry Regiment (35th), commanded by Colonel Henry G. Fisher, would strike west along the Mason Road toward Much'on-ni. In the centre, the 5th RCT would attack west along the southern access road to Chinju, launching from Chindong-ni and aiming to merge with the 35th at Much'on-ni. Also jumping off from Chindong-ni, the 5th Marines would attack along the south coastal road to the town of Kosŏng, before striking northwest to Sach'ŏn via Changchon.

To the rear of the UNC offensive, the 1st and 3rd battalions, US 24th Infantry Regiment (1/24th and 3/24th), assisted by the regiment-sized ROKA Task Force Min, was tasked with securing the hilly mass of the Sŏbuk-san area, which sat in between the lines of attack of the 35th and the 5th RCT.

While Task Force Kean's plans were being debated and finalized, the KPA 6th Division was already moving eastward to seize Pusan. Several thousand KPA troops were also firmly ensconced in commanding positions at Sŏbuk-san. On the eve of the American assault, the KPA 6th Division strength stood at 7,500, including the 83rd Motorized Regiment, KPA 105th Armoured Division, on attachment. In support would be 36 artillery pieces and 25 tanks.

At 6.30 a.m. on the morning of 7 August, the 35th's 2nd Battalion (2/35th) initiated Kean's attack at The Notch, three miles southwest of Chungam-ni. Here, some 500 KPA troops, with self-propelled guns in support, clashed with the Americans. After a bitter engagement lasting several hours, the 2/35th took the pass and high ground to the north.

By last light, the 35th had attained their westward objective at the Much'on-ni road junction. Together with air support, Fisher had accounted for 350 of the enemy, while destroying two T-34 tanks, a Soviet-made SU-76 self-propelled gun and five anti-tank guns. Early the next morning, Fisher consolidated his position to wait for the arrival of the 5th RCT on his left flank.

To Fisher's rear, however, the US 24th Infantry Regiment, under new commander Colonel Arthur S. Champney, found it difficult to clear the broken terrain around Sŏbuk-san of elements of the KPA 6th Division. The day before Kean had launched his offensive, the North Koreans had ambushed L and I companies to the west of Haman, killing 12 Americans and causing the rest to flee in disarray.

To the south at Chindong-ni, by the evening of 6 August the 5th RCT had relieved the US 27th Infantry Regiment on the front line to the west of the town. On higher ground to the north, the 2nd Battalion, 5th Marines (2/5th Marines), took up jumping-off positions, while the 1st Battalion, 5th Marines (1/5th Marines), replaced elements of the 27th in reserve. That night, KPA troops, after clearing the spur below Fox Hill of a platoon from the 2/5th RCT, assumed a commanding position overlooking both the 5th Marines and 5th RCT command posts, American gun emplacements, and the main supply route to Chindong-ni.

Following a 20-minute artillery barrage, at 7.20 a.m. on 7 August the 1st Battalion, 5th RCT (1/5th RCT), set off westward to the road junction that would take them southward to Kosŏng. However, the battalion failed to follow the designated route, and stopped on a hill feature three miles short of where they had meant to dig in to cover the advance of the 5th RCT and the 5th Marines.

At 11 a.m. that morning, Lieutenant Colonel Harold S. Roise led the 2/5th Marines toward the spur at Fox Hill to relieve Lieutenant Colonel John L. Throckmorton's 2/5th RCT. In debilitating temperatures in excess of 40°C, the Marines failed to clear the spur of enemy troops, sustaining six times more heat-exhaustion casualties than from KPA fire.

Confusion ensued, in which communication lines were disrupted and the 27th in reserve became involved in the mêlée. Eventually, by 11.20 a.m. the Marines took over the front-line positions from the 27th. Instantaneous orders were received from Kean, immediately giving command of all ground troops on the Chindong-ni front to Brigadier General Edward A. Craig, commanding officer of the 1st Provisional Marine Brigade.

A 105mm howitzer of an American divisional field artillery battalion (FAB).

At first light on the morning of 8 August, 2/5th Marines stormed Fox Hill on the heels of an airstrike. Despite strong resistance from KPA 6th Division troops, the Marines took the position and relieved F Company, 5th RCT. D Company sustained eight killed and 28 wounded.

It was by now abundantly clear to Kean that his forces had clashed with the advancing KPA 6th Division across the entire Masan–Chindong-ni front. While his task force fought their way westward, just to the north of Chindong-ni elements of the KPA had seized Hill 255 during the night of 7 August. The feature commanded the main road to the rear to Masan, at which point the North Koreans had blocked the road.

With the failure of the 2/24th and 3/5th Marines to dislodge the North Koreans in heavy fighting, B and C batteries of the US 159th Field Artillery Battalion discharged 1,600 rounds at the KPA stronghold, supported by elements of the US 555th 'The Triple-Nickel' FAB firing 105mm howitzers. Airstrikes and tank and mortar fire joined the attack, but it would not be before noon on 9 August that the 3/5th Marines and troops from the 24th secured Hill 255. The North Koreans had suffered an

An American M2 4.2-inch mortar in action. (Photo Sgt Guy Kassal)

estimated 600 casualties, including 120 confirmed killed. In the final assault, 3/5th Marines' casualties amounted to 70, with at least half to heat exhaustion. H Company lost 16 killed in action and 36 wounded.

Kean's next priority was to take the strategic hill at the Kosŏng road junction that the 1/5th RCT had failed to secure. This task was given to Throckmorton's 2/5th RCT, battered and exhausted from the trauma that was Fox Hill. Throckmorton could only muster two companies, G and E, but with the support of three tanks and M2 4.2-inch 'Goon Gun' and M1 81mm mortars, on the night of 9 August, his men took the hill feature. Only now could Kean refocus his energies on the delayed westward offensive.

On the afternoon of 9 August, 1/5th Marines marched on Kosŏng, the original coastal road objective. Progress was swift and largely unhindered as 1st Marine Air Wing Vought F4U Corsairs from the carriers USS *Sicily* and USS *Badoeng Strait* provided rapid-response air support when any KPA threat appeared.

Late morning on the 11August, the US 1st Battalion, 11th Marines artillery laid down a barrage on crossroads to the west of Kosŏng as 3/5th Marines neared the town's outskirts. The bombardment produced an unexpected bonus for the Americans when their action flushed out units of the KPA 83rd Motorized Regiment, 105th Armoured Division that had been waiting nearby, concealed under camouflage netting. Breaking cover, the North Koreans made the decision to retire to Chinju via Sach'ŏn, fleeing Kosŏng in a diverse 200-vehicle convoy, comprising trucks, jeeps and motorcycles laden with troops, ordnance and ammunition, and supplies.

Four Corsairs from the *Badoeng Strait*, already overhead on a reconnaissance sortie, immediately set about strafing the column at low level. Retaliatory North Korean ground fire hit two of these iconic gull-winged workhorses of the Pacific theatre, causing one to crash. Shortly thereafter, a second wing of Corsairs and USAF F-51 Mustangs continued to wreak havoc on the sitting column of North Korean vehicles. Advancing troops on the ground discovered 31 trucks, 24 jeeps and 45 motorcycles either ablaze or rendered unserviceable by the successive American airstrikes. Tons of equipment and ammunition lay abandoned or destroyed.

Early the next morning, commanding officer Lieutenant Colonel George R. Newton took 1/5th Marines through the 3rd Battalion to lead the Marine brigade west to Sach'ŏn, a short eight miles from the objective of Chinju. Within four miles of Sach'ŏn, at Changchon, elements of the KPA 83rd Motorized and 2nd battalion, 15th Regiment sprung an ambush on the Americans. A fierce firefight ensued, lasting

Corsairs taxi on the flight deck of the aircraft carrier USS *Badoeng Strait*. (Photo US Navy)

well into the evening. Carrier borne Corsairs provided valuable air support, and by late afternoon, troops of the 1/5th Marines had secured hills 250 and 301 to their right, and Hill 202 to the left.

During the night, North Korean troops overran two B Company platoon positions on Hill 202, resulting in 12 killed, 16 wounded and nine missing in action, presumed killed. As the new day dawned, the remaining Marines on Hill 202 were ordered to withdrew and retire toward Masan.

Elsewhere, on 10 August the 5th RCT on the middle prong was heading for Much'on-ni and a rendezvous with the 35th Infantry Regiment. By the primitive hamlets of Pongam-ni and Taejong-ni, North Koreans were dug in on a long ridge to the north of the main east–west road. To the west of the two settlements, two ridges stretched for about a thousand yards before converging like an inverted V, in what the Americans referred to as 'the Gulch'. Running along the base of the southern ridge, the main road then climbed out of the valley and through a pass commanded by the KPA. The northern ridge stood above its neighbour.

At this time, the 2/5th RCT had secured the southern ridge at Pongam-ni, while two companies of 1/5th RCT occupied the eastern reaches of the northern ridge. Establishing its HQ in Pongam-ni itself, A and B batteries of the 555th FAB established gun emplacements on the peripheries of the two villages. Augmenting these two batteries to the north of the road, was the understrength 90th FAB. Slightly eastward and to the rear of Pongam-ni, 5th RCT had established its HQ, flanked by C Battery of the 555th FAB.

On the night of 10/11 August, the North Koreans commenced a simultaneous and sustained attack on the American infantry and artillery positions. At first light, airstrikes enabled the embattled Americans to stand their ground and push the North Koreans back into the hills.

Colonel Ordway's priority was to now move his regiment out from their vulnerable situation and through the pass toward Much'on-ni. Lieutenant Colonel T. B. Roelofs now assumed command of 1/5th RCT from the badly wounded and evacuated Colonel Jones. Arriving at regimental HQ at 2 p.m. on the 11 August Roelofs was immediately tasked with clearing the ridge to the north of the road and to secure the pass. In holding this position, the 1/5th RCT would cover the combat team as it moved westward away from Pongam-ni and through the pass.

As the sun started setting, B and C companies of 1/5th RCT, with weapons and artillery of 2/5th RCT in meaningful support, took on the North Koreans on the northern ridge, and as darkness fell, B Company secured a commanding position north of the pass. Content with his battalion's apparent success, the exhausted Roelofs set up his tactical HQ, before creeping under his jeep and falling asleep.

Despite his concerns about superior North Korean strengths in the vicinity of the pass, the reluctant Ordway was obliged to comply with Kean's urgent instructions to move west with all possible haste. The task force commander was himself under considerable pressure from US Eighth Army HQ, where Walker required the Chinju Pass line to be secured and held so as to release the Marine Brigade and the 5th RCT for urgent deployment elsewhere.

At 9 p.m. that night, Ordway received a divisional signal ordering him to immediately move Throckmorton's 2/5th RCT and a battery of artillery through the pass. The remainder of the regiment would follow the next morning. Ordway struggled to suppress a strong sense of foreboding by trying to placate his misgivings through a belief that division HQ knew more than he did of the enemy placements.

By midnight, Throckmorton and C and HQ batteries of the 555th FAB had cleared the pass after having encountered only light North Korean resistance. However, the commander had now lost radio contact with regiment HQ below. Isolated, he could neither call for assistance nor react to any similar request.

At around 1 a.m. on 12 August, Roelofs was woken up to be informed that radio contact had been lost with C Company on the northern ridge, from where it could clearly be heard that the Americans were under heavy attack. Roelofs, fearing a massed KPA attack, urged Ordway to immediately move the formed-up combat team through the pass. But the RCT commander was adamant that he would follow divisional orders and wait for first light. Taking two of his officers with him, Roelofs drove toward Pongam-ni, where he found the regiment's convoys and the 555th FAB ready and awaiting the order to move out.

Parties sent out to re-establish communications with C Company had either gone missing or had failed to find the troops. From his HQ in the valley, Ordway soon caught sight of 1/5th RCT troops streaming down the ridge as they fell back from the KPA attack. With the North Koreans now clearly holding the high ground over his regiment, Ordway needed no further cajoling from Roelofs. He would be a sitting duck when daylight came, so at around 4 a.m. he eventually acquiesced and gave the order to move through the pass. The rear echelons and supporting cadres would head the column, followed by the artillery, with 1/5th RCT bringing up the rear.

However, what should have been an orderly and efficient 20-minute passage through the pass, quickly developed into a jam of vehicles that inched forward at a snail's pace. As the sky started getting lighter to the east, the North Koreans opened fire on the column. By sunrise, and with the 1/5th RCT holding the pass, Ordway finally left the valley.

The C ration is the most acceptable ration we have in use in Korea. Everyone likes it. The relative acceptance ratings of the meat items are: (1) beans and frankfurters; (2) beans with pork; (3) meat and beans; (4) ham and lima beans; (5) spaghetti and meat; (6) hamburgers with gravy; (7) pork sausage patties with gravy; (8) meat and noodles; (9) chicken and vegetables; (10) beef stew; (11) corned-beef hash.

This ration is a combat ration, and one of its characteristics is its capability of being consumed hot or cold. The reaction of the men was that the only items acceptable cold were the three bean items. The principal complaints were against the meat-and-spaghetti and the meat-and-noodle combinations. Both items were too dry, and when heated they would burn. The hamburgers and the sausage patties had too much fat and too much gravy. It is difficult to determine the acceptance of the chicken and vegetables.

In the C-4 and the C-6 we had a chicken-and-vegetables combination. The men disliked it. We had previously received reports on this, and in the C-7 we have a product of the same name but from a different formula. The men interviewed who have eaten the C-7 reported that the acceptance on the chicken-and-vegetables was very high. It is a very good product.

The corned-beef hash and the beef stew had very low acceptance ratings. Part of this can be attributed to the f act that, when operations started in Korea, we had a limited stock of meat items to be issued in the B ration.

Supply Bulletin 10-495 has the menus we had planned to use, but we didn't have the items in stock. We had quantities of beef stew and corned-beef hash on hand, so they were shipped. The men had corned-beef hash and beef stew; beef stew and corned-beef hash. So the principal objection to the corned-beef hash in the C ration is that it has become the Spam of the Korean campaign. Beef stew—well, too much fat; very poor acceptance when cold.

It had been reported previously that there was too much meat in the C ration. I found that for those men in the rear areas—those who used the ration only when they were making a movement—there may be too much meat. But we must remember that this ration was designed for the fighting man. He is a young man—old men cannot climb hills. Fighters work hard. They will eat practically all you can carry up to them.

Major Lawrence Dobson, Observer for The Quartermaster General, 25 April 1951
(Center of Military History, United States Army)

A North Korean column advances.

Monitoring the westward movement of his troops up from the Gulch, Roelofs was dumbfounded at the sight of an A Company platoon and the section of tanks that had been positioned on a road into Pongam-ni from the north to deter the KPA from using the route to infiltrate the RCT's positions. No orders had been given for them to withdraw, and although Roelofs stopped them from moving any farther westward with the rest of the column, the damage had been done and the consequences would prove disastrous.

With armour and self-propelled guns in close support, the 13th Regiment of the KPA 6th Division poured into the valley around Pongam-ni, striking brutally hard and virtually enveloping the 555th and 90th FAB emplacements. The Americans were no match, their howitzers incapable of being depressed low enough to have any effect on the closing North Koreans.

The rag-tag remains of Ordway's regiment, comprising mortar and heavy machine-gun platoons, fled out the valley. There was no opportunity to recover the dead. At around 10 a.m., with three tanks providing the rear guard, Roelofs' men finally came through the pass. Of C Company, only 23 men remained out of the original strength of 180.

It was estimated that soon after 9 a.m., the North Koreans had overrun the 555th FAB battery positions. The fate of the 90th FAB was nearly as catastrophic, but for the determined fighting of the artillery men and air support from F-51s allowing the survivors to extricate themselves from a desperate situation. Kean ordered the 3/5th Marines and 3/24th to fight their way toward Pongam-ni in an attempt to find survivors of the artillery battalions. However, both units were recalled before they reached the tragic scene, that would later be christened 'Bloody Gulch' by the American troops.

Here, two 555th batteries lost all eight of their 105mm howitzers, while A Battery of the 90th lost all six of its howitzers. At the time it was reckoned that as many as a hundred 555th men lost their lives at their gun emplacements, with another 80 wounded. The figures for the 90th were ten killed, 60 wounded and 30 missing.

The ultimate horror of the 12 August rout would only be discovered five weeks later when the Americans regained control of the area. In an abandoned house in Taejong-ni the remains of 55 men of the 555th FAB (24th Infantry Division) were discovered. They had been captured by the KPA 13th Regiment, taken into the house and machine-gunned to death. Not far away, the bodies of 20 men of the 90th FAB (25th Infantry Division) were found, each shot in the head. The massacre of 75 American POWs by North Korean forces was among the first in a series of

An armed F-51 Mustang of the Fifth Air Force ploughs through standing rainwater during takeoff to execute an airstrike against North Korean positions. (Photo US NARA)

atrocities, but more would follow: only five days after Bloody Gulch, 42 American soldiers of the 5th Cavalry Regiment taken prisoner by the North Koreans were executed, many with their hands tied behind their backs.

From this time, the various constituent elements of Task Force Kean started receiving orders to return toward Masan to the approximate positions from where the counter-offensive was launched on 7 August. In the afternoon of 16 August, Walker dissolved Task Force Kean, in the knowledge that it had failed in its objective to secure and hold the Chinju Pass line. Whilst many argued that the fighting capabilities of the KPA 6th Division had been underestimated, casualties inflicted by the task force on the North Koreans were not unsubstantial. For the US 25th Division, it was an essential baptism of fire in which much was also learned about the North Korean psyche.

Faced with the unforeseen setback presented by the failure of the Task Force Kean counter-offensive to take the strategic Chinju Pass, at Eighth Army HQ in Taegu commander Lieutenant General Walton Walker considered his defensive options. To the south of his left flank, Pang Ho San's KPA 6th Division, although weakened by recent action, remained a threat to the Pusan Perimeter generally and, more specifically, the Sŏbuk-san mountains overlooking the important north–south Komam-ni–Chindong-ni road. To the northwest of Komam-ni, the rugged P'il-bong spur, topped by the 900-foot Sibidang-san, commanded the surrounding terrain.

Seeking to bolster the defence line, Major General William Kean's US 25th 'Tropic Lightning' Division was moved into the area by 15 August.

The 35th 'Cacti' Infantry Regiment (35th), under Colonel Henry Fisher, established positions to the north of the line and west of Komam-ni to the Nam River. The 1st Battalion (1/35th) held the left flank, the second Battalion (2/35th) the right, along the Nam River, while the 3rd Battalion (3/35th) was held in reserve just to the south. In support, the 35th had the 64th FAB (105mm M2A1 howitzers), C Battery of the 90th FAB (105mm M114 howitzer) on attachment, and A Company of the 89th Tank Battalion, equipped with M4A3E8 'Easy Eight' Sherman tanks.

Colonel Arthur Champney's 24th 'Deuce Four' Infantry Regiment (24th)—one of the so-called 'Buffalo Soldier' regiments, largely made up of African-Americans—set up positions to the south on the eastern fringes of the Sŏbuk-san.

On attachment to the division, the 5th RCT, commanded by Lieutenant Colonel John Throckmorton, initially held the high ground commanding the Chindong-ni coastal road. The 27th Infantry Regiment (27th) remained in Eighth Army reserve. Also on attachment to the division were the 1st and 3rd battalions of the 29th Infantry Regiment (29th), respectively redesignated the 3rd Battalion, 35th Infantry Regiment (3/35th) and 3rd Battalion, 27th Infantry Regiment (3/27th).

DARKENING SCENE

Monday, August 14, 1950

The overall picture of the fighting in Korea is still far from reassuring, and though the American field command have been reluctant to admit that a further short-ening of the line will be necessary there are as yet no grounds for confidence that this will not be so. We observed here a week ago that the possibility of a Korean Dunkirk could not be ruled out. Nothing has happened in the intervening seven days to alter that view. The American counter-offensive on the southern front fell short of achieving the weight and momentum which first reports of the action encouraged; in fact, the operation appears to have suffered badly from the inadequacy of the United Nations forces engaged and the North Koreans' ability to switch their troops so as to cover their weak spots. The real danger now is in the Communist threat in the Pohang sector, where a successful drive down the coastline would put the United Nations forces in an almost untenable position. The question therefore arises: If America is driven out of Korea now and holds true, as she must, to her own Far Eastern interests and the interests of the United Nations by a re-invasion of the Korean peninsula, what will Russia do? Even if the men of Moscow have decided that, for the time being at least, they do not want to take the risk of starting a general conflict —for the shield of the atomic bomb still covers the Western democracies —they could, and undoubtedly would, seek to brand America as the aggressor. They could be counted upon to take full advantage of the loss of prestige that would inevitably follow an American withdrawal from Korea and the wide avenues for mischief which this would throw open to them. The best that the United Nations could hope for would be that an American Dunkirk at this time would result only in an intensification of Communist guerrilla warfare in Malaya, Indo-China, and Burma. The fuel, however, which such a situation would cast upon the fires already smouldering in various parts of the Far East might well touch off a major conflagration. It is, therefore, not surprising that Mr Churchill and Mr Clement Davies are pressing for an earlier recall of Parliament, and their proper anxiety at the seriousness of the world situation throws into sharp relief Mr Attlee's complacent reply that there is nothing in their letters to him that discloses "any particular reason" for this early recall. The Government have, in a crisis of this potentiality, a clearcut duty to keep the nation fully informed and alert, and it is hard to see what valid objection the Prime Minister can have to consulting Parliament earlier than September 12.

Hull Daily Mail, Monday 14 August 1950

From north to south, the 13th, 14th and 15th regiments of the KPA 6th Division faced the American-led UN forces with an estimated strength of eight and a half thousand. Included were South Koreans forcibly conscripted into the ranks. The 10,000-strong KPA 7th Division, comprising the 30th, 31st and 32nd regiments, was now also deployed to augment the KPA 6th on the Masan front.

Following several probing attacks on the US 25th Division's defensive lines, at 3 a.m. on 17 August, KPA artillery opened fire on the 1/35th command post in Komam-ni. An hour later, North Korean troops fell on A Company, effectively dislodging two platoons from their positions. At first light, B Company launched a counterattack, regaining ground lost during the night. The following morning, in what would become five days of fluctuating fortunes as the North Koreans persisted in their attempts to turn the 35th's left flank, A Company was forced back, only to retake their position in a counterattack.

On the night of 19/20 August, the 1/35th's artillery laid down a barrage of around 200 shells an hour against the tenacious North Korean attacks. That morning, C Company of the 35th and A Company of the former 29th moved out to straddle the Komam-ni road in support of A and B companies on the Sibidang observation point. The North Koreans immediately challenged this move, but it was only with deliberate artillery fire and airstrikes that the KPA troops were beaten off, losing an estimated 350 men.

Early on 22 August, KPA infantry, without preparatory artillery and mortar fire, launched a heavy attack on the 1/35th position, breaching the battalion's defences by cutting the perimeter barbed wire. Three battalion companies engaged the North Koreans in bitter close-quarter combat, with both sides employing small arms and grenades. A Company, after being dislodged, regained its position after three hours of fighting.

The following day, the North Koreans broke off their assault on the 35th at Komam-ni. Kean's divisional line had been successfully defended in the sector occupied by the 35th.

By mid-August, the 24th Infantry Regiment (24th) held the 25th Division's centre line of defence, a 13,000-yard-long stretch of broken, hostile terrain—the Sŏbuk-san—characterized by jagged and often precipitous ridges, punctuated with forbidding mountains such as hills 743 and 665, the latter given the moniker 'Battle Mountain'. In the latter half of August, the summit of Battle Mountain would change hands 19 times, during which the 24th sustained more than 500 casualties. The bald peak was of significant strategic value to both antagonists, providing as it did commanding views of both the KPA-held valley and the 24th's command post at Haman.

On the morning of 18 August, elements of the KPA 6th Division overran E Company of the 2/25th on the northern spur of the mountain, killing the company commander. The following day, the North Koreans also dislodged C Company from

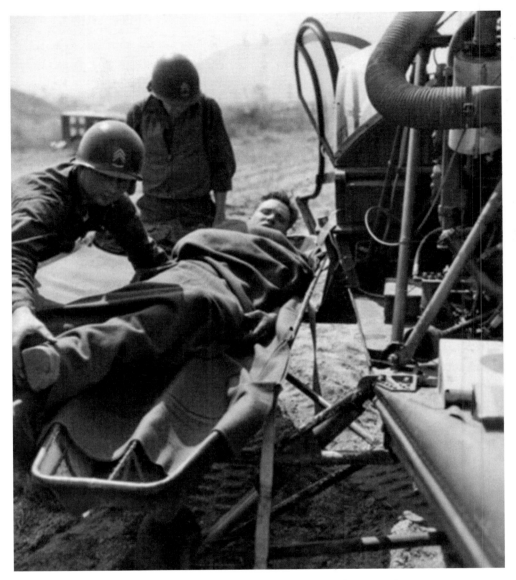

Medical evacuation by helicopter of a wounded American soldier. (US NARA)

the peak. Now an all-too-common scenario, the American officers found it virtually impossible to regroup the routed company to full strength to retake their position. The majority of the South Korean police who had also fled the summit, were as problematic. A yawning mile-long gap in the 24th's line was rapidly exploited by the North Koreans.

On the 20th, as the KPA launched another determined attack on the Americans, most of C Company ran from their positions, leaving behind the company commander and 25 men. Hearing that the company had been overrun, galvanized the Americans into a massive counterattack. Batteries of the 25th's 159th FAB and mortar teams bombarded the enemy positions, while air support flew 38 sorties, hitting the mountain with napalm and fragmentation bombs, rockets and machine-gun fire. All this achieved, however, was to force the remainder of C Company and elements of E Company off the mountain. From numerous 24th positions on the Sŏbuk-san, desertions continued in worrying acts of blatant disobedience.

Throckmorton's 5th RCT was now also brought into the fray, as 1/5th RCT attacked and secured the mountain's southern approaches on 21 August, only to be driven off that night. At noon the next day, the 1/5th RCT went back up, and after five hours of vicious fighting, B Company took the highest ridges. The Americans, however, under constant KPA attack, were not able to consolidate their positions. Just to the north, L Company of the 24th vacillated, constantly falling back to I Company's base position at the slightest sign of KPA aggression. The two companies lost any semblance of being cohesive combat units, resulting in their total withdrawal on 24 August. The onerous task of holding the mountain now rested with C Company and a platoon from E Company, together with a company of South Korean police.

On 27 August, the 3/24th relieved the 1st Battalion in the area, but the seeming perpetual cycle of attack, withdraw and counterattack continued well into September. American strategy now became one of containment of the KPA on Battle Mountain. K Company of the 24th and C Company from the 65th Engineer Combat Battalion established a fortified position to the east and below the mountain, from where observers directed howitzer and mortar fire onto the KPA stronghold. During the impasse, the 5th RCT was moved out for more pressing demands on the perimeter. In this no-win period on the Sŏbuk-san, on the night of 31 August elements of the KPA 6th Division attacked Lieutenant Colonel Paul F. Roberts's 2nd Battalion, 24th Infantry Regiment (2/24th) at its position on the crest of a ridge one mile west of Haman. As the South Koreans abandoned their positions at the Chungam-ni–Komam-ni pass, the KPA fell on 2/24th's F Company, capturing an American M20 75mm recoilless rifles which they used to knock out two American tanks. Just to the south, KPA T-34/85 tanks struck at E Company. All along the 2/24th line there was only token resistance. Yet again desertion was prevalent as the GIs fled toward Haman. The battalion's command post was overrun, and the unit ceased to be an effective combat force.

The North Koreans now threatened to envelope Haman. Battalion commander Roberts failed to muster even a handful of troops to make a defensive stand. Champney was forced to translocate his regimental command post two miles down Engineer Road, a supply route to the northeast of Haman. C Battery, 159th FAB

American troops in Korea fire an M20 75mm recoilless rifle. (Photo US Army)

followed, with barely sufficient time to recover their howitzers. Despite efforts by the Americans to bring in elements of the 27th and 35th infantry regiments to plugs the holes left by the fleeing 1st and 2nd battalions of the 24th, at first light on 1 September an estimated two regiments from the KPA 6th Division were seen streaming into a blazing Haman.

Kean, anxious to avoid another unsustainable setback, appealed to Eighth Army HQ for the immediate deployment of their whole 27th Infantry Regiment reserve to his line. Walker, however, only released the 1st Battalion (1/27th) under Lieutenant Colonel Gilbert J. Check, supported by a platoon from the regiment's Heavy Mortar Company, a platoon of B Company, 89th Tank Battalion (M4A3E8 Shermans), and A Battery, 8th FAB (105mm howitzers).

On his arrival at the 24th's command post two miles east of Haman mid-morning on 1 September, Check waded into total pandemonium. Troops of the 1st and 2nd battalions, 24th, refused to muster, even when threatened by armed military police. Check could barely move in the quagmire of retreating vehicles, equipment and soldiers.

The US 27th Regiment command post under a bridge at Haman. (Photo US Army)

Eventually at 2.45 p.m., American F-51 Mustangs and Lockheed F-80 Shooting Stars conducted a half-hour bombing and strafing of KPA positions around Haman. At 4.30 p.m., following an artillery bombardment, Check with tanks from A Company, 79th Tank Battalion, attacked and retook Haman with comparative ease. However, from a nearby ridge to the west, a strong force of North Koreans poured machine-gun fire into the advancing Americans, resulting in many casualties. Undaunted, Check pressed home his attack, striking west of Haman to clear the adjoining ridges of North Koreans and pressing toward the 24th's former positions.

The 24th Infantry Regiment was organized on November 1, 1869 from the 38th and 41st Infantry Regiments. All the enlisted soldiers were black, either veterans of the U.S. Colored Troops or freed slaves. From its activation to 1898, the 24th Infantry served throughout the Western United States. Its missions included guarding posts, battling Indians, and protecting roadways against bandits.

1898 saw the 24th Infantry deploy to Cuba as part of the U.S. Expeditionary Force in the Spanish-American War. At the climactic battle of San Juan Hill, the 24th Infantry assaulted and seized the Spanish-held blockhouse and trench system on the hill. In 1899 the Regiment deployed to the Philippine Islands to help suppress a guerrilla movement. The Regiment would return to the Islands again in 1905 and 1911. In 1916 the 24th Infantry guarded the U.S.-Mexico border to keep the Mexican Civil War from spilling on to U.S. soil. When it did, the 24th joined the "Punitive Expedition" under General Pershing and entered Mexico to fight Pancho Villa's forces.

In 1919, rebels and troops of the Mexican government fought in Juarez, Mexico, which borders the U.S. City of El Paso, Texas. The 24th Infantry crossed over again to engage the rebels, ensuring that no violence erupted across the U.S. border.

During World War II, the 24th Infantry fought in the South Pacific Theater as a separate regiment. Deploying in April 1942, the Regiment assumed defensive positions in the New Hebrides Islands. The 24th moved to the Solomon Islands, including Guadalcanal, and secured airfields for the protection of incoming personnel and supplies. In the spring of 1944, the 1st Battalion, 24th Infantry (Deuce-Four) was attached to the 37th Infantry Division and fought on Bougainville Island. Later the battalion was attached to the Americal [23rd Infantry] Division. The entire 24th Infantry, when reunited, occupied Saipan and Tinian Islands from December 1944 to July 1945. At the end of the war, the 24th took the surrender of forces on Aka Shima Island, the first formal surrender of a Japanese Imperial Army Garrison.

From the end of World War II through 1947, the 24th occupied Okinawa, Japan, after which it relocated to Gifu, Japan. On February 1, 1947, the Regiment reorganized as a permanent regiment of the 25th Infantry (Lightning) Division. In late June of 1950, soon after North Korea invaded South Korea, the 24th deployed to Korea to assist in what was initially termed a "minor police action." The 24th Infantry fought throughout the entire Korean peninsula, from the defense of the "Pusan perimeter" to its breakout and the pursuit of communist forces well into North Korea, to the Chinese counteroffensives, and finally to U.N. counteroffensives that stabilized near the Demilitarized Zone.

It was inactivated on October 1, 1951.

(US War Department, US National Archives & Records Administration)

The whole of the next day, 135 sorties of US aircraft kept the North Koreans from regrouping for a counterattack. Some fighters came from as far away as the Yellow Sea where the carriers USS *Valley Forge* and USS *Philippine Sea* were making way at full speed toward Masan. At noon Check retook the 2/24th's positions abandoned two days previously.

The North Koreans returned at dawn on 3 September, but aided by tank, artillery and mortar fire, the 1/27th stood their ground, while KPA casualties neared a thousand. As darkness fell on 4 September, reconstituted elements of 1/24th and F Company from 2/24th relieved Check's exhausted men, who retired to a defensive position just to the east of Haman. Regimental commander Champney established a fresh 24th command post in the centre of the town, with H Company providing protection.

The following morning, before sunrise, two companies of North Koreans attacked. Catching H Company unawares, the Americans fled without offering any resistance. Two machine guns were abandoned, which the KPA troops employed to fire on

On the aircraft carrier USS *Valley Forge* Grumman F9F-2 Panthers and Vought F4U-4B Corsairs are readied for air support sorties over Korea. (Photo US Navy)

Champney's command post. In desperate close-quarter fighting, the North Koreans were finally turned back a scant hundred yards from the command post.

On 6 September, while touring front-line defences, Champney sustained a severe gunshot wound from a North Korean sniper. He was immediately evacuated and 3/24 commander, Lieutenant Colonel John T. Corley, assumed command of the troubled, segregated 24th Infantry Regiment. The next day, the North Koreans, after launching a final attack on Haman and beset with major troop shortages, gave up any hope of retaking Haman.

In the 25th Division's line, simultaneous North Korean attacks threatened the 35th along the Nam River to the northwest of Haman. Just before midnight on 31 August, a KPA Soviet-made SU-76 self-propelled gun of the KPA 7th Division started firing into the 35th's G Company across the river. With artillery in close support, a regiment of North Koreans then crossed the Nam to attack F and G companies. Other KPA troops crossed the river to the north of Komam-ni at the boundary of Lieutenant Colonel John L. Wilkins, Jnr's 2/35th and Lieutenant Colonel Bernard G. Teeter's 1/35th. As the North Koreans landed on the south bank and started firing, a contingent of 300 South Korean police, placed there to warn of a KPA attack, fled in all directions. As the North Koreans split left and right to take on G and C companies respectively, a large force, instead of moving toward Komam-ni as anticipated, veered off to the east to come up to the rear of 2/35th.

Under cover of an artillery barrage, two battalions from the 13th Regiment, 6th KPA, then attacked 2/35th positions on the Sibidang-san high ground, while KPA tanks, self-propelled and anti-tank guns moved on Komam-ni at the base of Sibidang-san. On the crest of the rise itself, B Company infantrymen withstood the North Korean onslaught, but by 2.30 a.m. the Americans were running dangerously low on ammunition. To B Company's rear, at the base of the mountain, a platoon from C Company scaled the steep sides to resupply their comrades with ammunition.

By first light, it had gone quiet in front of B Company. The North Koreans had disengaged and abandoned any designs on the American stronghold. On the slopes over which they had been traversing, the Americans discovered huge amounts of equipment discarded by the North Koreans as they withdrew, including 33 machine guns. They also came across the body of the KPA 13th regiment's commanding officer.

Also on 6 September, the 1/27th and 2/27th commenced clean-up operations to the south of 2/35th, which elements of the KPA had penetrated after circling behind Sibidang-san. Caught between the two US regiments, the North Korean losses were heavy.

Over the next fortnight, attacks by the dispirited North Koreans on the 35th's positions along the Nam River's south bank were desultory and ineffective, and would no longer pose any threat to this section of Walker's left flank.

A Soviet-made ZPU-4 anti-aircraft machine-gun mount with four 14.5mm guns captured from the North Koreans during the Naktong battles on display in the Yŏngsan War Museum. (Photo rheo1905)

The US 25th Infantry Division's casualties in the Masan sector amounted to 138 killed, 646 wounded and two taken prisoner. Most of the 5th RCT's casualties suffered in the defence of the Pusan Perimeter were at Masan: 269 killed, 573 wounded and four missing.

The North Koreans had sustained much greater losses and thousands were taken prisoner. The KPA 7th Division had lost 60 percent of the 10,000 strength with which it had commenced operations against the UN perimeter. The 6th KPA had lost 80 percent. Total North Korean forces had been reduced from around 20,000 to 6,000 by the end of the battle for Masan.

The comparative conduct in combat between the US 24th and 35th regiments was poles apart. Division was compelled to arrest 116 deserters from the 24th during that

A US merchant vessel unloading mail at Pusan. (US Army)

August, while only 15 from the 27th and 12 from the 35th were detained on the same charges. US 25th Division commander Kean, seeing the 24th as weak and a danger-ous liability, called for the regiment to be disbanded and its men absorbed into other units in the perimeter. Walker, however, refused to entertain any such suggestions. On the other hand, the 35th had acquitted themselves so admirably that they were nominated for a Presidential Unit Citation (originally called the Distinguished Unit Citation), awarded for "gallantry, determination, and *esprit de corps* in accomplishing its mission under extremely difficult and hazardous conditions".

For the remainder of the defence of the Pusan Perimeter, neither the North Korean nor the UN forces would come even close to claiming victory over the other. However, and at great cost, the North Koreans had been forced to repeatedly call off their offences to take Masan and withdraw. Conversely, UN forces had been able to attain their immediate strategic objective of holding the perimeter's southern flank.

2. THE NAKTONG BULGE

At 317-miles long and with a catchment in excess of 9,000 square miles, the Nakdong River is the longest in South Korea. Known at the time of the Korean conflict as the Naktong, the north–south stretch of the river formed most of the western line of the Pusan Perimeter, before doglegging to the east and finally disgorging into the East Sea at Pusan. Up to several hundred yards wide as it nears its estuary, the Naktong provided a natural defensive barrier for the UN forces squeezed into a square tract of real estate to the southeast of the Korean peninsula by the North Korean People's Army.

Ten miles north of Masan, the west–east stretch of the Naktong marked the line-of-defence boundary between Major General William B. Kean's US 25th Infantry Division and the US 24th Infantry Division commanded by Major General John H. Church. For a distance of 16 miles along the river, Church's grossly understrength division—its combat efficiency just over 50 percent— and elements of the Republic of Korea Army (ROKA) were tasked with keeping the North Koreans out of Walker's defence perimeter.

To the west of the town of Yŏngsan, the Naktong flows in a great loop that, with some notoriety, became the Naktong Bulge salient of the Korean War. UN force numbers were insufficient to comprehensively protect the commanding ground to the east of the river line. Observation points and listening posts would play a key role in the early detection of North Korean forces across the Naktong. In the event of a breach, Church would draw forces from elsewhere in the line to contain and repel the enemy offensive.

With an aggregate divisional strength of only just over 12,000, Church had to extend his men along a 34-mile front when tactical doctrine called for nine miles. From the northern extreme of the sector, the 2,000-strong ROKA 17th Infantry Regiment held a 30,000-yard line. The next 12,000 yards was the responsibility of the 21st Infantry Regiment (21st) supported by the 14th Engineer Combat Battalion. To the northwest of Pugong-ni, the Heavy Mortar Company covered the next sector downstream to the commencement of the bulge in the Naktong. In isolated positions separated by unavoidable gaps along a 16,000-yard front, the division's 34th Infantry Regiment (34th) faced the bulge. I, L and K companies of the 3rd Battalion, 34th Regiment (3/34th) held the regiment's front from north to south, with the 1st Battalion, 34th Regiment (1/34th) in regimental reserve to the rear at Kong-ni. The 19th Regiment was Church's divisional reserve to the north at Ch'angnyong.

To the west of the bulge, KPA 4th 'Seoul' Division (KPA 4th) commander, Major General Lee Kwon Mu had, by the beginning of August 1950, established his command post at Hyŏpch'on. The 40-year-old, Manchurian-born Lee, a combat veteran of the Communist Chinese Eighth Route Army, had undergone officer training in the Soviet Union. After the capture of Seoul on 28 June and battle successes down the peninsula, including the routing of the US 24th Infantry Division at Taejon in mid-July, the *Inmun Gun* (North Korean armed forces) general had overnight been elevated to the lofty status of a great hero. Personally decorated with the *Chosun Minjujui Inmum Kong-whakuk* (Hero of the Democratic People's Republic of North Korea) and the *Chosen Kukki Hunjang* (Order of the National Flag, First Class), Lee's division was also bestowed with the honorary title 'Seoul' by North Korean leader Kim Il-sung. In the first week of August, Lee still had 7,000 combat-tried troops at his command.

A minute after midnight on 6 August 1950, Lee ordered the firing of a red and yellow flare as the signal for 800 members of the 3rd Battalion, KPA 16th Regiment to lead the advance across the Naktong toward the ferry stage at Ohang on the east bank. With the majority of the troops stripped naked, their uniforms and weapons held above their heads, the North Koreans silently commenced their shoulder-high wade through the river.

Exploiting a gap between the unsuspecting I and L companies of the 34th—Church had anticipated an enemy attack farther north—the North Koreans thrust deep into

The Soviet-made SU-76 self-propelled gun employed by the North Koreans was the second most-produced Soviet armoured vehicle of the Second World War, after the ubiquitous T-34 tank. (Photo Alexxx1979)

the Naktong Bulge salient, repelling an attempt by elements of the 1/34th to halt their advance, in which C Company suffered 50 percent casualties. During the night of 6/7 August, the ROKA 17th did in fact frustrate an attempt by the North Koreans to cross the Naktong in their sector.

By 8 p.m., the North Koreans had penetrated three miles east of their bridgehead on the Naktong, about half way to Yŏngsan. Church then ordered the 1st and 3rd battalions of the 19th Infantry Regiment (1/19th and 3/19th) to attack the KPA's left flank to the north of the 34th. In a village a mile east of the river, elements of the 19th enveloped 300 KPA troops, killing most of them.

Reacting on the morning of 7 August, Walker replaced the ROKA 17th with the eponymous Task Force Hyzer. Commanding officer of the 3rd Engineer Combat Battalion, Lieutenant Colonel Peter C. Hyzer, was placed in command of the task force which, in addition to his own battalion, comprised a light-tank company—without tanks—and the 24th Reconnaissance Company. Walker also reduced the US 24th Division's front by deploying the US 1st Cavalry Division on Church's right flank. But by now the North Koreans had taken Cloverleaf Hill to the north of Tugok and Obong-ni Ridge to the south of the road to Yŏngsan, threatening both Yŏngsan and Miryang and therefore the integrity of the Pusan Perimeter's left defence line.

That same day, at 4 p.m. the newly arrived and well-equipped 9th 'Manchu' Infantry Regiment, US 2nd Infantry Division, was moved into the sector. Having only arrived at Pusan from Fort Lewis, Washington, on 31 July, Church immediately ordered the fresh, but untried, 1st and 2nd battalions (1/9th and 2/9th) to attack the KPA in the area of Tugok. However, the inexperienced Americans, many of them reservists, were stalled by the North Koreans after having only gained a tenuous toehold on Cloverleaf Hill. For the next three days, both sides inflicted heavy casualties on the other as strategic positions were repeatedly gained and lost in a cycle of fluctuating fortunes in which neither achieve a decisive advantage over the other.

Taking a trick from Soviet combat practices, the North Koreans constructed 'underwater' bridges through the Naktong to facilitate the crossing of heavy vehicles, armour and artillery. By the morning of 10 August, an estimated two regiments of Lee's KPA 4th Division were dug in on the east bank.

For Church, it had become an imperative to destroy the KPA bridgehead, so at this time he rapidly assembled a large force with which to task this objective. Named Task Force Hill after the commanding officer of the 9th Regiment, Colonel John G. Hill, in addition to his own regiment, less its 3rd Battalion, the force included the 19th and 34th infantry regiments and the 1st Battalion, 21st Infantry Regiment (1/21st), together with support artillery. However, Hill was totally ineffective against the fortified KPA positions and artillery in the salient, and by nightfall, the whole North Korean 4th Division had crossed the Naktong and was moving south, outflanking Task Force Hill.

The next day, elements of the KPA commenced the North Korean assault on Yŏngsan, straddling the important supply route to the east of the town. To counter the threat, on 12 August Walker threw part of the 27th Regiment, US 25th Division, from their defence line south of the bulge, north to repulse the North Korean move on Yŏngsan. This was followed the next day by the dispatch of further reinforcements, the 2/27th and 3/27th pushing closer to the town, where they met with the 1/21st and the newly arrived 1/23rd of the US 2nd Division. The supply route was secured once more, and the North Koreans forced back to their stronghold on Cloverleaf Hill.

Through 14 and 15 August, Task Force Hill and the North Koreans continued to engage in fierce fighting that resulted in significant casualties being sustained on both sides. Just after midnight on 15 August, the KPA fell on the 1/21st before spreading their attack across the front and infiltrating the 2nd Battalion, 9th Infantry

US Marines take cover behind the hull of an M26 Pershing while the tank commander scans the road ahead. (Photo US Marine Corps)

Regiment (2/9th), 2nd Infantry Division's lines. The following day, the North Koreans also gained ground by pushing back the 2/19th and the 1/34th.

On 17 August, Walker disbanded Task Force Hill and committed the 1st Marine Provisional Brigade to the battle, moving the unit from combat in the Masan sector and attaching it to the US 24th Division. Commanded by General Edward A. Craig USMC, and with the nickname the 'Fire Brigade', the brigade comprised the 5th Marine Regiment (5th Mar), under Lieutenant Colonel Raymond L. Murray, an artillery battalion and a company of tanks.

Around this time, Lee's KPA 4th Division started to falter. His three regiments had now suffered major casualties in fierce fighting with the Americans for control of Cloverleaf and Obong-ni. Reinforcements were received, but in the form of untrained and unarmed South Koreans pressganged into service from surrounding villages. Lee's logistics had been stretched to breaking point as American air interdiction continually harassed any North Korean movement across the Naktong. Food and ammunition were scarce commodities, with Colonel Chang Ky Dok's 18th Regiment holding Obong-ni Ridge, not having received any resupply of ammunition since 14 August.

HEADQUARTERS, 1ST PROVISIONAL MARINE BRIGADE, FLEET MARINE FORCE

c/o FPO, San Francisco, California
From: Commanding General
To: Chief of Staff, United States Army
Subj: Special Report, Destruction of Enemy Tanks
23 Aug 1950

1. Three (3) enemy T-34/85mm tanks attacked our position (43.3–87.2), at 172005 August. Enemy tanks were moving northeast along road toward our position and were under attack of Air Force P-51 aircraft. The tanks were not stopped by the air during the attack.
2. The enemy tanks fired approximately four (4) rounds of HE ammunition at our troops without results. The enemy came under fire of our tanks, 76mm Recoilless Rifles and 3.5" Rocket Launchers almost simultaneously. Three (3) M-26 [Pershing] tanks moved 900 yards southwest down the road and positioned themselves overlooking a curve in the road. Two (2) of our tanks were abreast and opened fire at a range of 100 yards as the first two (2) enemy tanks came around the curve in the road.

3. The first M-26 fired two (2) rounds of APC [armour-piercing capped] ammunition at each of the enemy tanks, a total of six (6) rounds. All rounds fired at the hull penetrated the enemy armor.

4. The second M-26 tank fired one (1) round of APC ammunition at the first enemy tank; one (1) round of HVAP [high-velocity armour-piercing] and two (2) APC at the second tank and four (4) rounds of HE ammunition at the third enemy tank. Our second tank fired the HE ammunition through a penetration made previously by APC ammunition through the machine gun bow mount, front slope plate of the third enemy tank.

5. All enemy tanks were penetrated by APC ammunition when fired at the hulls. Approximately fifty percent (50%) of all tank rounds were fired successfully at the hulls, the remaining rounds at the turrets, which were not penetrated. All enemy tanks were burning at 2015, and although two (2) rounds were fired by the enemy at our tanks, [both] were misses.

6. During the tank attack 75mm Recoilless Rifles and 3.5" Rocket Launchers successfully damaged the enemy's tanks. The first enemy tank was hit by four (4) rounds of Recoilless Rifle fire and halted; the right track of the second enemy tank was hit and blown off by 3.5" rocket fire at a range of 75 yards and set on fire. As a result the second enemy tank ran into a ditch. The Recoilless Rifles fired four (4) rounds of ammunition at the first tank; one (l) round each at the second and third enemy tanks all at ranges of 100 yards. Rocket 3.5" hit all enemy tanks.

7. Although hit by 75mm Recoilless Rifles and 3.5" Rockets the enemy tanks continued firing and only one (1) was completely immobilized. One enemy crewman attempted escape from enemy tank No. 2, and three crewmen from No. 3; all were killed by small arms fire.

8. No Marine aircraft participated in the attack on the enemy tanks since the Tactical Air Coordinator (airborne) called planes off to prevent endangering our troops.

9. The Commanding Officer, 1st Battalion, 5th Marines, who received the attack stated that credit for one (1) tank should go to the 75mm Recoilless Rifles; one (l) to the tanks, and the remaining enemy tank to the Recoilless Rifles, 3.5" Rocket Launchers, and the tanks. He further stated that the 75mm Recoilless Rifles and the 3.5" Rocket Launchers are effective anti-tank weapons available to the Marine infantry battalion.

E.A. CRAIG

[Brigadier General Edward A. Craig, CO 1st Provisional Marine Brigade]
(RG 127, United States Marine Corps, NARA)

After midnight on 17 August, commanding officer of the 2nd Battalion, 5th Marines (2/5th Mar) assembled in front of Obong-ni Ridge in preparation for an attack on the high ground. Their sister battalions, 1/5th Mar and 3/5th Mar would follow the 2/5 Mar in that order.

Out at sea, 18 bombed-up F-4U Corsairs were launched from the American carriers *Badoeng Strait* and *Sicily*, scrupulously timed to arrive over Obong-ni Ridge after a massive bombardment by US 24th Division artillery.

As the choking dust and smoke dissipated, at 8 a.m. D and E companies, 2/5th Mar, numbering 120 Marines, attacked the ridge. As the Americans strode through paddy fields, North Koreans below the ridge hit them with a hail of automatic rifle fire. On reaching the base of the ridge, mortar bombs exploded among them as they desperately and agonizingly started to climb in the direction of the crest. Only two-thirds of Second Lieutenant Michael J. Shinka's 3rd Platoon, D Company reached the top. The Marines were immediately forced to seek cover from incoming enemy machine-gun fire and hand grenades in deserted KPA foxholes. The platoon immediately sustained five casualties.

An American M2A1 105mm howitzer static display, Camp Nihonbara, Japan. (Photo Hunini)

Knowing that to remain in this untenable position would result in the certain annihilation of his platoon, Shinka ordered his men back down. Half way down the ridge, his fellow Marines dragging the wounded as they went, Shinka paused to radio the D Company command post to ask for air support and extra men to have another go at taking the crest. Shinka linked up with other platoon commanders on the slopes of the ridge as Marine Corsairs once more bombed the North Korean positions, augmented by salvos of shell fire from tanks below. As the bombardment ceased, the Marines again tried to reach the crest. Shinka's 3rd Platoon was now down to nine combat-able men.

The North Korean reception on the crest was even more vicious, with two more of Shinka's platoon falling. Shinka was then hit in the jaw, so he could only motion with his hands for his decimated platoon to fall back. While ensuring that no one was left behind, Shinka took another bullet, this one in his arm.

At 3 p.m., the Marine attack on Obong-ni Ridge was abandoned, having lost 23 killed and 119 wounded in the attempt to take the feature. An hour later, A and B companies of Colonel George R. Newton's 1/5th Mar relieved what remained of 2/5th Mar.

However, the repeated ground and air attacks on Obong-ni Ridge had exacted a terrible toll on the North Koreans. Colonel Chang Ky Dok's KPA 18th Regiment had sustained an estimated 600 casualties during the day, and in the absence of medical supplies, his command was literally haemorrhaging to death. On nearby Cloverleaf Hill, the KPA 16th Regiment was ordered to deploy a battalion to replenish Chang's losses.

By means of a captured American SCR-300 radio, the beleaguered Chang was fully aware that the 1/5th Mar had relieved the 2/5th at the base of the ridge, as well as the fresh positions of Marine companies positioned on an outcrop a distance up the slope. Also a product of Soviet military schooling and a veteran of combat in China, Chang knew that he had to either take the initiative or face certain envelopment and defeat. As daylight waned, Chang made the decision to take the fight to the Marines below.

Earlier that day, after his Marines' attempts to take Obong-ni Ridge had ended in abysmal and costly failure, Colonel Murray became conscious of the imperative to neutralize the North Korean hold on Cloverleaf Hill before returning to the Obong-ni stalemate. Late in the afternoon, the 2/9th dislodged the North Koreans from Cloverleaf, allowing the American 1st and 3rd battalions, 34th Regiment, and 1st and 2nd battalions, 19th Regiment relative unhindered freedom of movement to surge into the bulge to the north.

At 2.30 a.m. on 18 August, Chang launched his attack on the unsuspecting Marines. Screaming while firing automatic assault rifles and lobbing grenades, the North Koreans breached the A Company, 1/5th Mar line, before crashing into B Company's defence perimeter where the attack stalled. While A Company withdrew down the slope, for almost an hour B Company was engaged in a frightful firefight that claimed many casualties on both sides—but the line held. The light of a new day revealed the bodies of around

American troops man an M1919 Browning .30 calibre medium machine gun on high ground. (Photo Ondrejk)

200 North Koreans, their decimated 18th Regiment gone from the battlefield. With Corsairs providing close air support, A Company pursued the remnants of the defeated KPA regiment, finally securing the ridge. The Marines suffered 50 percent casualties.

As 1/5th Mar moved southeast mopping up the Obong-ni Ridge, 3/5th Mar raced westward to engage the fleeing KPA 4th Division as it reached the Naktong. American howitzers and tactical aircraft pounded the broken North Korean force.

Early on 19 August, the pursuing Marines and GIs converged on the east bank, where all that remained in the bulge were Lee's 34 artillery pieces and countless rifles and machine guns, together with a miscellany of heavy equipment. They also left behind 1,200 dead for the UN forces to inter. It was estimated that Lee's division had been reduced to a little over 3,000 troops.

For the Americans, it was also a costly victory. The 9th Infantry Regiment and supporting units sustained 57 killed, 106 wounded, two captured and 13 missing, the 21st Infantry Regiment 30 killed and 70 wounded, the 19th Infantry Regiment 450 casualties, the 27th Infantry Regiment 150, and the 34th Infantry Regiment about four hundred. The 1st Provisional Marine Brigade reported 66 dead, 278 wounded and one missing.

SECRET

SPECIAL ACTION REPORT
"A" Co., 1st Tank Battalion, attached to the 5th Marines
17 August 1950

The platoon was still in process of replenishing ammunition at 2000 when three enemy tanks were reported approaching the lines. In a matter of seconds the platoon was on the road moving forward.

The first section loaded 90mm APC [armour-piercing capped], upon order from the platoon leader, before rounding the bend in the road at the morning line of departure. Immediately upon rounding the bend the lead tank [M26 Pershing] came face to face with an enemy tank at a range of 100 yards. Tank 34, the lead tank, fired three rounds of APC, scoring one hit in the turret and two in the front slope plate. These set the tank on fire and put it out of action.

Tank 33 was ordered into position on the right flank of tank 34 which, due to lack of room, placed these tanks hub to hub. This movement was necessary in order to have at least two of our tanks in position to concentrate fire on the three enemy tanks.

The second enemy T-34 tank came into view at a range of 100 yards and tanks 33 and 34 fired 1 HVAP [high-velocity armour-piercing] and 5 APC at it, scoring 1 hit in the turret with the HVAP, and five APC hits in the front slope plate. These set the tank on fire, but because it was still directing fire against our troops the commanding officer of the 1st Battalion [5th Marines Regiment] ordered the tanks to continue firing on it. The two tanks fired 1 HVAP, 2 APC and 4 HE [high-explosive] into the right rear side of the turret.

The third enemy tank moved up behind the first and second tanks and the fire from tanks 33 and 34 was shifted to it. Five rounds of APC were fired and five hits were made on the front slope plate. The third tank was on fire after the second round hit the slope plate, and after the last one, was completely destroyed.

After destroying the third enemy tank the platoon was ordered to withdraw to the forward CP [command post]. During the tank battle, the first section received machine-gun fire and at least fifteen near misses from an unknown caliber anti-tank weapon.

(RG 127, United States Marine Corps, NARA)

A North Korean soldier captured by Marines during the fighting in the Naktong Bulge. (Photo US Marine Corps)

At his front HQ in Kimch'ŏn, northwest of the US Eighth Army HQ at Taegu, KPA Supreme Commander (of the Defence of Seoul) Ch'oe Yong-gŏn scrutinized the latest re-routed Soviet intelligence, the contents confirming a build-up of American forces on the east bank of the Naktong. Under Ch'oe's command were the KPA I Corps, led by war veteran Lieutenant General Kim Ung and the KPA II Corps, commanded by

Chinese Eighth Route Army veteran Lieutenant General Kim Mu Chong. I Corps covered the frontline extending from Waegwan, some 15 miles northeast of Taegu, and south to the Korea Strait. The II Corps front ran from Waegwan eastward to P'ohang on the peninsula's east coast. All told, Ch'oe was able to muster an estimated 98,000 troops, made up of 13 infantry divisions, one armoured division and two armoured brigades. One hundred new T-38/85 tanks had also recently arrived from the north. It was Ch'oe's intention to launch an all-out offensive—likely his last opportunity to breach the line—along the full length of the UN's over-extended Pusan Perimeter.

On 20 August, he issued attack orders to his two corps commanders. To KPA I Corps would fall the task of attacking and collapsing the perimeter in its sector, with nine infantry and one armoured divisions at its disposal. The KPA 1st, 3rd and 13th divisions were to break the American line at Taegu, held by the 1st US Cavalry and the 1st ROKA divisions; the KPA 6th and 7th divisions were to penetrate the US 25th Division line to the south; and the KPA 2nd, 4th, 9th and 10th divisions were to neutralize the US 2nd Division and strike farther east via Yŏngsan to sever the Americans' main supply route along the Pusan–Taegu road. The KPA 105th Armoured Division was also attached to the corps.

KPA II Corps was to employ its 5th and 8th divisions to destroy the ROKA 6th and 8th divisions east of Taegu, while the KPA 5th and 12th divisions would penetrate the eastern corridor at P'ohang by breaking through the ROKA 3rd and Capital divisions.

While Ch'oe was of the firm belief that discovering and exploiting a weak spot somewhere on the perimeter would work in his favour, he would focus his resources once more on the Naktong Bulge. The strategic significance of a successful ingression into the salient and through the American lines demanded his full attention.

By this time, US 2nd Division, commanded by Major General Laurence B. 'Dutch' Keiser and with only seven infantry battalions, had relieved the US 24th Infantry Division, with the US 2nd Division's 9th Regiment (9th)—minus the 3rd Battalion which was defending the airfield at Yŏnil—establishing itself on the high ground west of Yŏngsan, holding a sector of 20,000 yards, including the bulge.

The 3rd Battalion, US 23rd Regiment, had also been removed and attached to the 1st Cavalry Division in the Taegu sector. The 23rd Regiment (23rd)—less the 3rd Battalion—held the line to the right of the US 9th. Three companies of the 1st Battalion, 9th Regiment (1/9th) held the southern half of the regiment's sector, while the 2nd Battalion, 19th Regiment (2/19th) held the northern half. A full-strength 1st Battalion, 23rd Regiment (1/23rd) had been placed in the line, while the 2nd Battalion (2/23rd)—minus E Company which had been seconded to the US 9th as an additional reserve—was held in reserve. The US 38th Regiment (38th) had placed two companies beyond the bulge and two on the regimental flank. The 3rd Battalion (3/38th) was held in reserve.

On 28 August, Lieutenant General Kim Ung issued KPA 2nd (Major General Lee Ch'ong Song), KPA 4th (Major General Lee Kwon Mu), KPA 9th (Major General Pak Kyo Sam) and KPA 10th (Major General Kim Tae Hong) divisions with orders for the imminent offensive on the Naktong Bulge, specifically tasking the KPA 9th Division with outflanking and eliminating the American presence in the bulge by taking Miryang and Samnangjin, thereby cutting off their route of supply and withdrawal. However, the North Koreans were not aware that the newly arrived US 2nd Division had replaced the battered US 24th Division in the bulge.

On the southern extreme flank of the US 9th's Naktong River line, just above the confluence of the Nam and Naktong rivers, on a ridge culminating in Hill 94 and which ran parallel to the Naktong, A Company, 1/9th, had dug in. At the base of Hill 94 was the hamlet of Agok, 300 yards from the Kihang ferry stage on the Naktong's east bank.

On the evening of 31 August, A Company moved off the ridge to take up positions close to the river. Two M26 Pershing tanks and two M19 gun motor carriages

An American M19 gun motor carriage with twin 40mm Bofors captured during the Korean War on display in Beijing. (Photo Morio)

(MGMCs), the latter armed with twin 40mm Bofors guns, established a position close to the ferry under the command of Sergeant Ernest R. Kouma.

At around 8 p.m., dense fog descended on the Naktong in eerie silence, but the tranquillity of the warm night was short-lived. An hour or so later, the loud detonations of North Korean artillery shells and mortar bombs landing on the east bank shattered the silence all along the bulge line. To the west of Yŏngsan, an understrength G Company took SU-76 fire from the west bank, while the E and F company positions came under heavy rifle and machine-gun fire from their front.

At 10.30 p.m., Sergeant Kouma's four vehicles opened fire on a pontoon bridge being constructed across the river by the North Koreans, destroying the structure. Soon afterwards, Kouma received a signal ordering him to withdraw with the rest of A Company. On their way out, North Koreans in American army uniforms ambushed Kouma's patrol. Wounded, Kouma was left stranded with his tank. Undaunted, he held the Agok position until 7.30 a.m. the following morning, at which time he fought his way through North Korean-held terrain for eight miles. Kouma would receive the Medal of Honor for his gallantry.

By midnight, the KPA 9th Division had crossed the Naktong into the bulge in several places, while the KPA 2nd Division overran the 23rd's C Company. Having been pushed back to their original line defence positions, A Company regrouped and dug in for the night.

Five miles to the north, where B Company held Hill 209 overlooking the Paekchin ferry stage, the reinforced regimental reserve E Company, dubbed 'Task Force Manchu', was preparing to conduct a raid into the KPA-held west bank of the Naktong. With D and H weapons' companies of the US 9th providing supporting fire, elements of the 2nd Engineer Combat Battalion would ferry the task force across the river.

However, as the D and H company commanders moved their men and guns up the slopes of Hill 209 to establish suitable emplacements, the North Koreans struck, and the Task Force Manchu mission aborted. Pushed onto a knob below Hill 209, the two weapons' companies sat out the night, half a mile from B Company's perimeter above.

The KPA 10th Division had simultaneously attacked the 38th's line during the night, overrunning E and F companies. Having avoided the KPA at Paekchin, E Company had been ordered east to set up a blocking position in the pass in between Cloverleaf Hill and Obong-ni Ridge on the road to Yŏngsan. However, at around 3.30 a.m., the company was ambushed as they advanced down the road, resulting in heavy casualties including the company commander who was killed.

At first light, the men of D and H companies discovered that B Company had been routed, with substantial casualties, and the whole area was now swarming with North Korean troops striking east. In spite of retaining radio communications with his battalion, H Company's Lieutenant Edward Schmitt realized that they were on their own will little chance of succour. Having seen sufficient evidence of the North Koreans executing American prisoners, for Schmitt surrender was not an option. For the rest of the day and into the night, the trapped Americans fought off concerted KPA attacks. An attempted resupply ended in water containers bursting as they hit the ground with most of the drop falling into enemy hands. The next day, Schmitt was wounded, but even as KPA machine-gun fire raked his position, the Americans would not capitulate. That night, the North Koreans again sent in their infantry to attack the rapidly dwindling group of combat-fit GIs. Ammunition, food and water was all but exhausted, but miraculously the isolated Americans remained undefeated to see the sun rise on the third day.

Elsewhere in the line, by mid-morning on 1 September, US 2nd Division commander Major General Keiser received the news at his HQ in Muan-ni, 7seven miles east of Yŏngsan, that the North Koreans had bisected his division: the 23rd and the 38th regiments to the north, so far untouched but out of contact with division HQ, and to the south, the US 9th, collapsing under the sheer ferocity of the enemy attack. Having created a six-mile-wide corridor, the North Koreans now held Cloverleaf Hill and Obong-ni Ridge and were threatening Yŏngsan.

GENERAL ORDERS

Number 66
Headquarters, 2d Infantry Division
APO 248 c/o Postmaster
San Francisco, California
16 October 1950

AWARD OF THE SILVER STAR
By direction of the President, under the provisions of the Act of Congress approved 9 July 1918 (WD Bul 43, 1918) and pursuant to authority contained in AR 600-45, the Silver Star for gallantry in action is awarded to the following named officers and enlisted men:

COLONEL WALKER R GOODRICH, 018815, (then Lieutenant Colonel), Artillery, United States Army, a member of Headquarters, 2d Infantry Division Artillery, displayed gallantry in action on 1 September 1950 in the vicinity of Changnyong, Korea.

During this period, the enemy's continuing ground offensive threatened to break through American defensive positions along the Naktong River in the central sector of the Korean Front. At the height of the enemy offensive, Colonel Goodrich went to the front lines to obtain a better picture of the situation. While en route he discovered a large gap in the front lines which contained no friendly forces and through which enemy troops had begun to move.

He observed that a short distance to the south of this gap there were friendly tanks and infantry troops. Although under constant enemy fire, he personally led these forces to the vicinity of the breach and directed their efforts in effectively closing the gap. His skilful employment of troops and his superior tactical knowledge of both tank and infantry units were of inestimable value in preventing the enemy from exploiting the breakthrough in the Naktong River salient.

The gallantry and superior leadership displayed on this occasion by Colonel Goodrich reflect great credit both upon himself and the Armed Forces of the United States. Entered the military service from New Hampshire.

LIEUTENANT COLONEL JOHN R HECTOR, 030717, Artillery, United States Army, Commanding Officer, 37th Field Artillery Battalion, 2d Infantry Division, displayed gallantry in action against an armed enemy on 1 September 1950 in the vicinity of Changnyong, Korea.

On this date, he was returning to his Command Post from a regiment supported by his battalion. His vehicle was suddenly subjected to intense direct small cross fire by a group of enemy soldiers who had infiltrated behind infantry units in that area. His driver was wounded in the initial burst of fire and stopped the vehicle. Colonel Hector, disregarding his own personal safety and ignoring the hail of small arms fire directed against him, carried the wounded driver to a position of safety about 200 yards to the rear. He then returned to the scene of the ambush, effectively returned the enemy fire, and forced them to withdraw. Recovering the vehicle, he placed the wounded man therein, and drove him to a nearby aid station.

The gallantry displayed by Colonel Hector in endangering his own life to save that of a fallen comrade great credit upon himself and is in keeping with the highest traditions of the military service. Entered the military service from California.

(US 2nd Infantry Division Orders GO-5, 1950, US Army, NARA)

American troops of the 9th Regiment, US 2nd Division, with M26 Pershing tank support, on the Naktong River. (Photo US Army)

Approaching the town from the south, the KPA engaged the US 2nd Division Reconnaissance Company and M26 Pershings from the 72nd Tank Battalion in a fierce firefight. As night fell, the North Koreans started to infiltrate the low ground to the south of Yŏngsan, attacking the 2nd Engineer Combat Battalion to gain the town. In the ensuing fight that raged until late morning, the battalion's D Company, commanding the town, inflicted severe casualties on the KPA assailants with rifle and machine-gun fire and by the very effective employment of 18 3.5-inch and 2.36-inch bazookas. D Company also paid heavily in its stubborn defence, with 12 killed and 18 wounded. The company commander was the only officer not hit. On the eastern edges of Yŏngsan, A and B companies of the 72 Tank Battalion took equal share of the Americans' fight to keep the North Koreans from marching through Yŏngsan to their key objective of Miryang.

On the afternoon of 2 September, 800 troops of the US 2/9th, with tanks in support, attacked through A Company, 2nd Engineer Combat Battalion (2/ECB), and by 3 p.m.

American troops prepare to fire an M9A1 2.36-inch 'Bazooka' rocket launcher. (Photo Sergeant Charles Turnbull)

had retaken the town. By last light, with Yŏngsan now cleared of the KPA, the 2/9th and A Company of 2/ECB held positions to the west and northwest of the liberated town. For the moment, the North Korean threat to Miryang had been neutralized.

Keiser now deemed it tactically necessary to treat his split division as two special force entities: division artillery commander Brigadier General Loyal M. Haynes to assume command of the northern group, dubbed Task Force Haynes, and assistant division commander Brigadier General Joseph S. Bradley in charge of the southern group—Task Force Bradley—comprising the 9th Infantry Regiment, the 2nd Engineer Combat Battalion and most of the 72nd Tank Battalion.

At US Eighth Army HQ, army commander Lieutenant General Walton Walker telephoned Major General Doyle O. Hickey, Deputy Chief of Staff, Far East Command in Tokyo, to appraise him of the critical situation along the Pusan Perimeter as the North Koreans tried to force his defence line at five points. The greatest threat was in the Naktong Bulge, especially along the US 2nd Division's boundary with the US 25th Division. He sought and received permission to commit the US 1st Provisional Marine Brigade to the bulge, and that same afternoon, Walker attached the brigade to his 2nd Division, and placed the 19th Infantry Regiment, US 24th Division, on standby. His fresh orders to the bolstered US 2nd Division were to eliminate all North Korean forces in the division's sector.

At a US Eighth Army Joint Operations Center (JOC) meeting, his ground forces now placed in the best possible positions to launch a counterattack, Walker looked to the US Far East Air Force (FEAF) for maximum possible air support. Acting commander of the US Fifth Air Force, Major General Edward Timberlake, telephoned FEAF vice commander, Major General Otto P. Weyland, in Tokyo. Timberlake informed Weyland of his intention to commit the Fifth Air Force in support of the US 2nd and 25th divisions, but requested the additional employment of Lockheed F-80 Shooting Star squadrons, currently stationed on defence duties in Japan. In support of his request, Timberlake reminded Weyland that the carriers *Badoeng Strait* and *Sicily*, hitherto invaluable providers of air support to Walker's US Eighth Army, had been called back to Japan to prepare for the Inch'ŏn invasion.

US Air Force Lockheed F-80C Shooting Star, armed with napalm bombs, takes off for a strike on the Naktong. (Photo US Air Force)

While the Miryang JOC deliberated with Tokyo, commander of UN forces General Douglas MacArthur was in conference with the respective commanders of US FEAF and US Fifth Air Force, Lieutenant George E. Stratemeyer and Major General Earle E. Partridge. MacArthur strongly recommended that Stratemeyer employ every aircraft at his disposal, including Boeing B-29 Superfortress heavy bombers, to assist Walker to beat off the latest North Korean offensive.

The carrier *Sicily* had already docked in Japan, so was not available. However, Corsairs off the *Badoeng Strait* were ashore at US Itami Air Base in Japan (Osaka Airport from 1959) and would be available to commence combat sorties over Korea on the morning of 2 September, after first flying to Ashiya Air Base for fuelling and arming. Two groups of B-29s were already bombed-up for interdiction carpet bombing, so were not available. However, 24 B-29s would be sourced from other bomb groups to be employed on 2 September against enemy targets in the towns of Chinju, Kŏch'ang and Kumchon.

Task Force 77, the fast carrier force of the US Navy Seventh Fleet, was at this time under steam in the northeastern Yellow Sea to conduct interdiction strikes north of North Korean-occupied Seoul. MacArthur signalled Commander Naval Forces, Far East, Vice Admiral C. Turner Joy, to render Walker's Eighth Army all possible support.

Within hours, US Fifth Air Force fighter-bombers were over the 40-mile front held by the US 2nd and 25th infantry divisions. The North American F-51D Mustang— the ubiquitous P-51 stalwart of the Second World War—many taken from storage, continued to dominate the air support element. Fitted with 5-inch rockets and a total of 1,000 pounds of bombs on two wing hardpoints, the Mustangs performed a ground-attack role rather than that of interceptor fighters.

Of the 167 close-support sorties conducted by the US Fifth Air Force on 1 September, 108 were against KPA forces attacking the US 25th Division's front south of the Nam River. The grateful division commander, General Kean, had positioned his Tactical Air Control Parties (TACPs) close to the front, from where forward air controllers could, with precision, identify and pinpoint enemy targets. This 'live' information would immediately be conveyed to a rudimentary Tactical Air Control Center, established within the 6132nd Tactical Air Control Group. Given the call sign 'Mellow Control', the radarless facility exercised control over all the TACPs in-country, in addition to providing the JOC with a radio network. Mellow Control would then disseminate enemy target information to North American T-6 Texan forward air control aircraft of the recently activated 6147th Tactical Control Squadron, Airborne, designated 'Mosquitos'. The centre also facilitated liaison with the 1st Marine Air Wing, however, in a clumsy protocol, all naval air strikes had to be coordinated from US Navy HQ in Japan.

Tactical Air Control Party (TACP) at the front. (Photo US Air Force)

Through the morning and early afternoon of 1 September, 59 US Fifth Air Force sorties were flown in support of US 2nd Division positions in the Naktong Bulge. In the afternoon, Task Force 77 launched 85 sorties from its carriers, but the contribution on the day was beset with logistical issues that reduced performance efficiency. As the task force carriers reversed course, maximum strike wings were launched while the designated target area was still 250 miles distant. With strict instructions to report to Mellow Control, scores of naval aircraft, already short of fuel after the long flight in, jammed the radio channels in their efforts to receive specific target data, including coordinates. The inevitable stacking as the aircraft queued to gain access to Mellow resulted in some running so low on fuel that they had to jettison their bombs and return to their carriers without making any contribution to the fight on the ground.

The next day, the KPA was relentless in its offensive all along Walker's perimeter. To the south of the bulge, the US 25th Division had stood their ground and were now launching counterattacks.

However, on their northern operational boundary, the US 2nd Division found it increasingly difficult to hold the line. The 1st and 2nd regiments of the KPA 9th Division, under Major General Pak Kyo Sam, in their first offensive of the campaign had forced the Naktong and were pushing toward Yŏngsan. Alarmingly, the 9th Infantry Regiment, US 2nd Infantry Division, lacked sufficient boots on the ground to defend the town.

3 September 1950
ASHIYA AIR FORCE BASE
At approximately 1030K the squadron [VMF-214] was alerted to move to Taegu, Korea. The move was to commence any time after 1400K but at 1250K the order was cancelled and the regular strike schedule resumed. The first three strikes, four Corsairs each airborne on the hour every hour beginning at 1300K, hit troop concentrations, gun positions, and supply vehicles while flying close support missions for the Marine Brigade on the Yongsan area. Similarly the four Corsairs of the 1649K strike worked over supply points and troop entrenchments in close support of a U.S. Army unit in the vicinity of Kagan-ni. Ordnance expended on the sixteen hops is as follows: sixteen full loads of 20mm ammo and one-hundred-twenty-five HVAR's [rockets].

4 September 1950
ASHIYA AIR FORCE BASE
With the exception of a one hour delay on the fourth hop, all five four-plane strikes were sent out on one hour intervals starting at 1130K. As on the previous day the primary mission of all strikes was close air support of the First Marine brigade. The first strike made rocket and strafing runs to rake retreating troops and knock out a tank at Kang-ni; the second strike duplicated this performance at Chir-hyon. Similarly the third and fourth strikes hit troops and machine gun emplacements near Kang-ni with the third strike also scoring hits on two tanks and a truck. The last strike of the day made numerous rocket and strafing runs on a troop concentration and a tank covered convoy of five trucks. Though successful in the attack on the enemy, one plane was shot up and the pilot forced to bail out. A helicopter operating nearby rescued the pilot unhurt in a matter of minutes after he had parachuted into enemy infiltrated terrain. One-hundred-fifty-nine HVAR's, eight 500-pound bombs, and the usual load of 20mm ammo [were] expended on the twenty sorties flown on this date.

(VMF-214 war diary, September 1950, US Army, NARA)

With a rout imminent, Keiser moved the 2nd Engineer Combat Battalion (ECB) to boost the 9th, while the US 72nd Tank Battalion and the division's Reconnaissance Company were repositioned closer to Yŏngsan. The 2nd ECB's A Company positioned themselves to the south of the Yŏngsan–Naktong River road, while D Company entrenched on the north side.

North Korean T-34 tanks destroyed by US Fifth Air Force airstrikes near Waegwan. (Photo US Army)

In a firefight lasting several hours, 300 KPA troops attacked A Company's position, the latter supported by M19 gun motor carriages of the 82nd AAA Battalion. Bradley immediately moved D Company to a hill overlooking Yŏngsan just to the south. A Company was then pulled back on to D Company's left flank.

In spite of poor weather conditions over the battle area, the Fifth Air Force was employing squadrons of aircraft released from their air defence duties in Japan. Together with the Marine air squadron, a total of 201 close-support sorties were flown. At the same time, 25 B-29s of the 307th Bombardment Group dropped 863 500-pound bombs on the towns of Kumchon, Kŏch'ang and Chinju. Personnel from Task Force 77 were deployed in front of the US 2nd Division to assist the Mosquitos with the coordination of carrier air support in this sector. With this development, Partridge dispensed with the requirement that naval aircraft had to report to Mellow.

Late on the afternoon of 2 September, while the 2/9th was clearing Yŏngsan, generals Keiser and Craig were in conference, planning a combined army/Marines counterattack for the next day. Elements of the Marine Brigade would attack along the Yŏngsan–Naktong main supply route (MSR) toward the familiar Cloverleaf/

Obong-ni hills. To the north, the 2/9th, supported by B Company of the 72nd Tank Battalion and D Battery of the 82nd AAA Battalion, were to establish contact with the beleaguered US 23rd Infantry. On the Marines left flank to the south, the 2nd Engineer Combat Battalion, what was left of the 1/9th, and elements of the 72nd Tank Battalion would fight their way to reconnect with the US 25th Division. Walker ordered the US 24th Division HQ and the 19th Infantry to move to Susan-ni, 15 miles east of the confluence of the Naktong and Nam rivers, and eight miles south of Miryang. From this assembly area, the units would be on permanent standby to support either the US 2nd or 25th divisions in the forthcoming counteroffensive. By this time, G and F companies of the 9th Infantry, together with A Company, 2nd Engineers, held the high ground to the west of Yŏngsan.

At 8.55 a.m. on 3 September, the 1/5th and 2/5th Marines commenced their attack to the west. Heavy enemy resistance was encountered the whole day, and by last light, the Marines dug in only two miles from Yŏngsan. The two battalions had sustained 191 casualties, including 34 killed.

A knocked-out US army truck with towed 105mm howitzer. (Photo US Army)

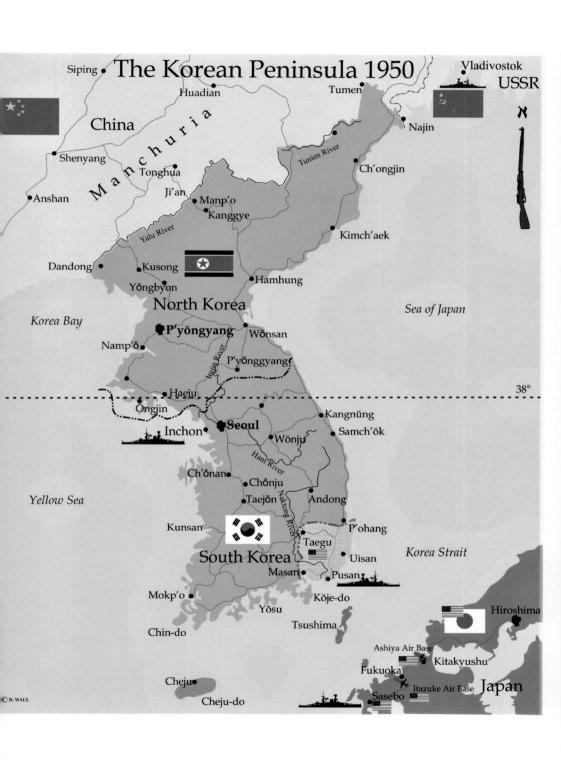

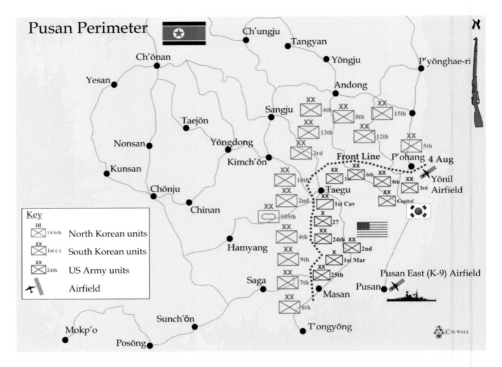

Pusan Perimeter

Key

North Korean units	14/6th
South Korean units	1st (-)
US Army units	24th
Airfield	✈

Shoulder Sleeve Insignia

US 2nd Infantry Division

US 24th Infantry Division

US Eighth Army

US 25th Infantry Division

US 1st Cavalry Division

Collar Badges

Armour

Chemical Corps

Intelligence Corps

Medical Corps

Transport Corps

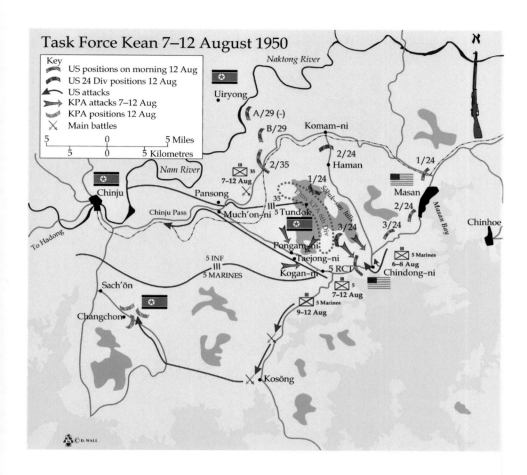

Task Force Kean 7–12 August 1950

Key
- US positions on morning 12 Aug
- US 24 Div positions 12 Aug
- US attacks
- KPA attacks 7–12 Aug
- KPA positions 12 Aug
- Main battles

5   0   5 Miles
5   0   5 Kilometres

Naktong River

Uiryong

A/29 (-)
B/29
Komam-ni
2/24
Haman
1/24

Nam River

2/35

35
7–12 Aug

Chinju

Pansong

Masan

2/24

3/24

3/24

Chinju Pass

To Hadong

Much'on-ni

5 Tundok

Elms KPA 6th Div
Sŏbuk-san hills

Masan Bay

Chinhoe

5 Marines
6–8 Aug
Chindong-ni

5 INF

5 MARINES

Pongam-ni

Taejong-ni
Kogan-ni

5 RCT

5
7–12 Aug

Sach'ŏn

Changchon

5 Marines
9–12 Aug

Kosŏng

© D. WALL

US Marines
cap badge

Vaught Corsair F4U flown by the US Marines 1950
in support of ground forces

KPA forces advance on Naktong Bulge 5–6 August 1950

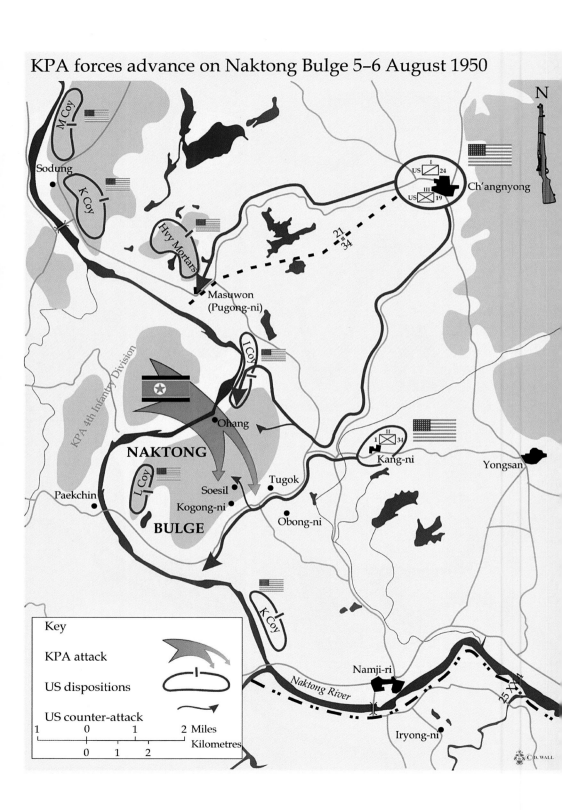

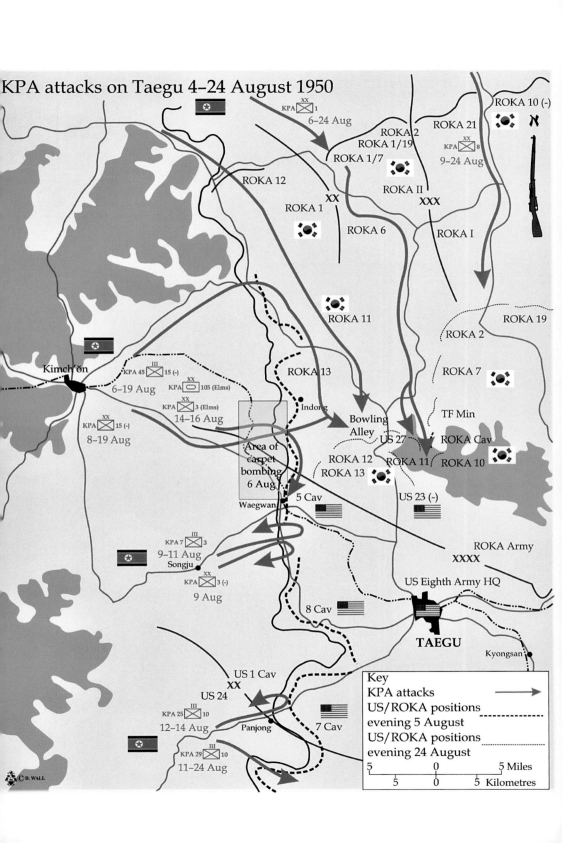

KPA attacks on Taegu 4–24 August 1950

ROKA 10 (-)

KPA ⊠ 1
6–24 Aug

ROKA 2
ROKA 1/19
ROKA 1/7

ROKA 21
KPA ⊠ 8
9–24 Aug

ROKA 12

ROKA II

ROKA 1   XX

ROKA 6   XXX

ROKA I

ROKA 11

ROKA 19

ROKA 2

Kimch'ŏn

KPA 45 ⊠ 15 (-)
6–19 Aug

KPA ▭ 105 (Elms)

KPA ⊠ 3 (Elms)
14–16 Aug

ROKA 13

ROKA 7

KPA ⊠ 15 (-)
8–19 Aug

Indong

Bowling
Alley

TF Min

US 27

ROKA Cav

Area of
carpet
bombing
6 Aug

ROKA 12

ROKA 13

ROKA 11   ROKA 10

Waegwan

5 Cav

US 23 (-)

KPA 7 ⊠ 3
9–11 Aug
Songju

ROKA Army
XXXX

KPA ⊠ 3 (-)
9 Aug

8 Cav

US Eighth Army HQ

TAEGU

Kyongsan

US 1 Cav
XX
US 24

KPA 25 ⊠ 10
12–14 Aug

Panjong

7 Cav

KPA 29 ⊠ 10
11–24 Aug

© D. WALL

Key
KPA attacks   →
US/ROKA positions   - - - - -
evening 5 August
US/ROKA positions   ·········
evening 24 August

5   0   5 Miles

5   0   5 Kilometres

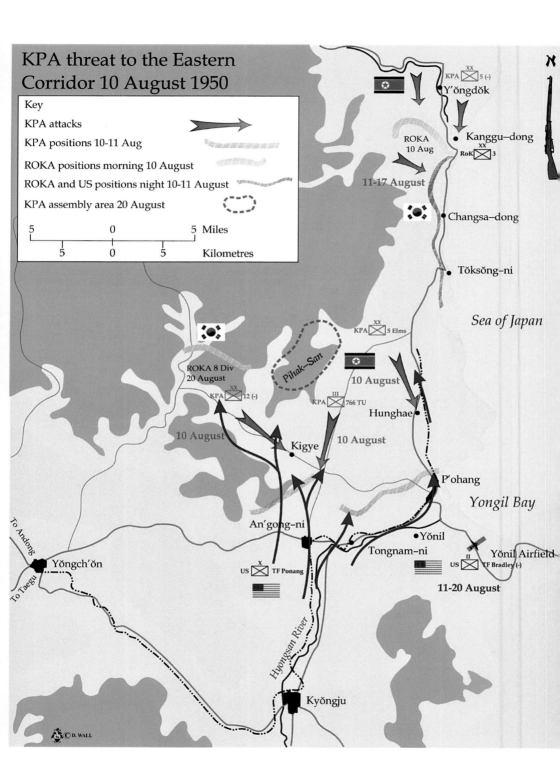

KPA threat to the Eastern Corridor 10 August 1950

Key

KPA attacks

KPA positions 10-11 Aug

ROKA positions morning 10 August

ROKA and US positions night 10-11 August

KPA assembly area 20 August

5 0 5 Miles

5 0 5 Kilometres

KPA XX 5 (-)

Yŏngdŏk

Kanggu–dong

ROKA 10 Aug

RoK XX 3

11-17 August

Changsa–dong

Tŏksŏng–ni

Sea of Japan

KPA XX 5 Elms

ROKA 8 Div 20 August

Pihak-San

KPA XX 12 (-)

KPA III 766 TU

10 August

Hunghae

10 August

Kigye

10 August

An'gong–ni

To Andong

Yŏngch'ŏn

To Taegu

US X TF Ponang

P'ohang

Yongil Bay

Yŏnil

Tongnam–ni

Yŏnil Airfield

US II TF Bradley (-)

11-20 August

Hyŏngsan River

Kyŏngju

© D. WALL

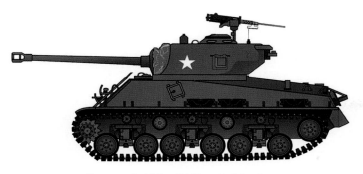

Sherman tank of C Coy, 70th Heavy Tank Battalion,
1st Cavalry Division near Chilgok, September 1950

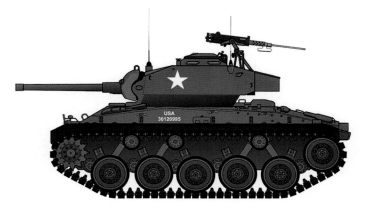

Chaffee M24

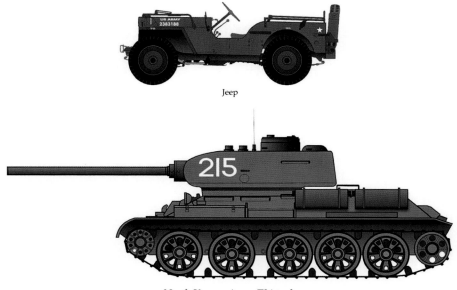

Jeep

North Korean Army T34 tank

Pusan remains of significant strategic importance to the American and South Korean navies. The ROKS *Hwacheon* (top) on exercises at Busan in October 2015, and the nuclear-powered aircraft carrier USS *George Washington* (CVN73) (below) pulls out of the port. (Photos ROK Forces and the US Navy)

During the day, the Fifth Air Force flew 249 close-support and 89 interdiction sorties in support of American ground forces, while 35 B-29s bombed KPA troop concentrations and equipment to the immediate rear of the North Korean lines. The participation in the counteroffensive by Task Force 77, however, was minimal. Partridge had received a signal from the carrier force informing him that urgent refuelling prevented it from assisting, and it was only with direct intervention from Tokyo that the fleet launched 28 sorties in support of ground troops in the Yŏngsan surrounds. This would be the last the Americans in the Naktong Bulge would see of the naval aircraft. For the next two days, the task force was diverted to attack targets in northwestern Korea, before returning to Sasebo base in Japan to prepare for the imminent amphibious assault at Inch'ŏn.

For three days, the KPA 9th Division and the much-depleted KPA 4th Division suffered major casualties as the Americans started to turn the North Korean offensive. While stragglers continued to hold the Cloverleaf/Obong-ni high ground, these two divisions had lost combat effectiveness.

At 8 a.m. on 4 September, after a very wet night, the 2/9th recommenced their attack on the east bank of the Naktong. As the troops advanced, there was ample evidence of a defeated enemy in retreat. Large numbers of North Korean corpses were testimony to the devastation that American aircraft and artillery had wrought on their ranks. Tons of equipment had been abandoned as the North Koreans fled, including two serviceable T-34-85 tanks.

That night, at around 10 p.m., an estimated two KPA companies failed to dislodge G Company from its hilltop position. However, a second attack followed soon afterward, forcing the Americans off the crest of the hill, but only as far as their support-tank positions. With the American armour clearing the crest with shell and machine-gun fire, G Company retook their positions, only to be beaten back once more. Undeterred, the Americans stormed back up the hill where bitter close-quarter and hand-to-hand fighting continued until first light, when American howitzers ensured that G Company would not again be dislodged from its strategic position.

On 5 September, the 9th Infantry repelled a KPA counterattack, while to their south the Marines, supported by elements of the 9th, 23rd and 38th regiments of the US 2nd Division, attacked the Obong-ni Ridge. It was now clear that the KPA 9th Division had lost its bite. The next day, MacArthur ordered the release of the 1st Marine Brigade from the Eighth Army back to Pusan.

To the north of the bulge, the US 2nd Division's 23rd Infantry, assisted by the 3/38th, took on and finally defeated the KPA 2nd Division. By this time, the 23rd Infantry's combat efficiency was down to 38 percent, but the North Korean division had expended all its available resources in its repeated attempts to break through the American line. However, it would take until 16 September before the Americans had fully neutralized the KPA threat in this sector.

0845 Hrs
The Regimental Commander issued an attack order in substance as follows: "Enemy forces to the front of the 23d Infantry Regiment are estimated to be elements of three Infantry Regiments; the 4th, 5th and 6th of the NKPA 2d Division, with a mortar regiment attached. Their orders are to hold their present positions at all costs. The 23d Infantry will attack and secure the high ground at 44.298.3, 44.1-99.1 and 44.1-97.8 [three commanding ground terrain features, to the 23d Infantry's front]. The line of departure will be from present positions, with the 37th Field Artillery direct support and Heavy Mortar Company in general support. The time of the attack is 1030 Hrs."

1008 Hrs
The Commanding Officer of the 2d Battalion requested that the attack be delayed 30 minutes, because of difficulties encountered in manoeuvring the 2d Battalion into position for the Jump-Off. His request was approved and all units concerned were notified.

1103 Hrs
The Attack jumped off.

1355 Hrs
All companies reached their objective by 1355 Hrs. Fox and Able Companies encountered extremely heavy resistance and suffered heavy casualties. More than once intense enemy mortar fire forced the companies to pull back until counter-battery could silence the mortars. Able Company suffered 60 casualties in this action. George Company was unable to attack until 1120 Hrs due to an intense barrage of self-propelled and automatic weapons fire. Major John Callum, Regimental S-2 [intelligence], was killed by enemy artillery fire, while manning an observation post. George Company was ordered to continue the attack, in order to gain control of a commanding ridge to its front. The objective was secured at 1600 Hrs.

1850 Hrs
George Company was hit by a heavy enemy counterattack and forced back to a ridge immediately to their rear.

1937 Hrs
An air strike during the afternoon, destroyed 15 enemy field pieces, 10 armored trucks and approximately 500 enemy troops.

2010 Hrs
The Regimental Commander reported to the Commanding General of the 2d Division, that, the attack had improved our positions, however, the Regiment

had suffered many casualties. During the remainder of the period the regimental positions were heavily shelled but the enemy did not resume the attack.

(23rd Infantry Regiment HQ war diary,
6 September 1950, US Army, NARA)

During their offensive against the Pusan Perimeter at the Naktong Bulge, the KPA 2nd and 9th divisions sustained a total of 10,000 losses. In its service in the defence of the Pusan Perimeter, including in the first battle of the Naktong, the US 2nd Infantry Division suffered 1,120 killed, 2,563 wounded, 67 captured and 69 missing in action. The 1st Provisional Marine Brigade suffered 185 killed and around 500 wounded, mainly at Yŏngsan.

What remains open to debate, however, is why the 7,000-strong KPA 10th Division did not enter the fray. Had it done so, the outcome in the bulge might well have been very different for Walker's Eighth Army. As it was, the general's HQ at Taegu came under increasing pressure from the North Koreans during this period.

North Korean prisoners of war.

A knocked-out KPA T-34, September 1950.

Above left: A South Korean propaganda leaflet.

Above right: A Korean child searches for her family as refugees flee south to escape the rampaging Communist forces. (Sgt D. Helms/ US Army)

North Korean propaganda poster. (USMC)

Victims of the Hill 303 massacre, with bound hands, at the burial area near Waegwan, 17 August 1950. (US Army)

A graphic North Korean propaganda painting showing Americans torturing a Korean woman.

Around 1,800 South Korean political prisoners were executed by the South Korean military at Taejŏn, over three days in July 1950. (Maj Abbott/ U.S. Army/ via AP Photo)

A giant C-119 Flying Boxcar transport of the US Far East Air Forces Combat Cargo Command roars in for a landing at an advanced airfield in Korea. This plane carries a load of seven and a half tons. It has just returned from dropping critically needed supplies to outnumbered American troops on the battle lines. (Department of Defense)

3. TAEGU HQ THREATENED

Early in July 1950, General Douglas MacArthur made the decision to place Lieutenant General Walton Walker, commanding the US Eighth Army, in control of ground operations in Korea. Arguably best known for his command of the US XX Corps during the Second World War, Walker immediately appointed Colonel William A. Collier as acting chief of staff in Korea, dispatching him to South Korea to identify a suitable site for his army headquarters. Walker's serving chief of staff, Colonel Eugene M. Landrum, would go to Korea at a later date.

Collier was no stranger to the peninsula, having completed tours of duty there in 1948 and 1949, first as deputy chief of staff and then as chief of staff of US army forces in South Korea. Collier's choice for Walker's HQ quickly fell on Taegu, apart from Pusan, the last remaining major South Korean city not held by the invading North Koreans. Situated in the northwest corner of the Pusan Perimeter, Taegu offered natural defences in the form of the Naktong River to the south and mountains to the north. A major transport nexus, the city also possessed a functioning cable relay station that had served the Tokyo–Mukden cable.

On 13 July, Walker arrived at his new HQ, the base of the Eighth United States Army in Korea (EUSAK). The Republic of Korea Army headquarters was also moved to Taegu from Taejon as the UNC forces were driven ever southward by the North Koreans. Four days later, the newly elected president of South Korea, Syngman Rhee, requested that ROKA, under Chief of Staff General Chung Il Kwon, fall under Walker's command.

South African Personal Representative of the UN Secretary-General, Colonel Alfred G. Katzin, formally handed Walker the United Nations flag, as confirmation that his role was in pursuance of a UN mandate. The combined US and ROKA force in his command numbered some 75,000 men, of which 58,000 were South Korean.

Activated in early July 1950, the ROKA I Corps assumed operations on the US 24th Division's right flank. Having clashed with superior KPA forces in the central mountains to the east of the Seoul–Taejon main road, the ROKA 1st, 2nd and Capital divisions of ROKA I Corps had been decimated to between 3,000 and 3,500 troops each. The whole corps now remained with only seven artillery pieces and around 30 81mm mortars, all without sights.

On 14 July, ROKA activated its II Corps. Headquartered at Hamch'ang, the corps comprised the ROKA 6th and 8th divisions and the 23rd Regiment. A final reorganization of ROKA occurred on 24 July: ROKA I Corps, made up of the ROKA 8th and Capital divisions, and the ROKA II Corps with the 1st and 6th divisions. The remnants

South Korean (ROKA) troops circumventing paddy fields. (Photo US Army)

of ROKA 2nd Division was absorbed by the ROKA 1st Division, while the ROKA 3rd Division was posted to the eastern corridor. By the end of July, the South Korean army had a combat strength of just on 86,000 men. From west to east along the front in the Taegu sector, the ROKA II Corps held the line to the east of the US 1st Cavalry Division, and ROKA I Corps to the right of II Corps.

In the American sector, from north to south, the US 1st Cavalry Division's 5th, 8th and 7th regiments were stretched out along the Naktong River south of Waegwan. On the American's right flank, the ROKA 1st Division faced the Suam and Yumak mountains to the north of Taegu. On its right flank, the ROKA 6th Division faced east in defence of a narrow valley that carried the Kunwi road into the Pusan Perimeter.

The US 1st Cavalry Division, like the US 24th on their left flank, had a very long front along the Naktong River to defend. To the west of Taegu, two battalions of the 8th Cavalry Regiment (8/Cav) each had a front of 10,000 yards. To the north at Waegwan, the 5th Cavalry Regiment's front extended for 14,000 yards. About 7,000 yards to the rear, divisional FAB batteries were emplaced, each 6–7,000 yards apart. Distances within

73

regimental sectors, however, precluded any single FAB from massing its battery fire. To compensate, rapid fire was the only alternative: during one battle, ten 105mm howitzers fired 120 shells in 70 seconds, an average rate of one shell every six seconds per gun.

To the UNC front, five North Korean divisions would assemble in an arc from Tŭksŏng-dong and around Waegwan to Kunwi: the 10th Infantry (Motorized), 3rd Infantry, 15th Infantry, 13th Infantry and 1st Infantry divisions. In support was the KPA 105th Armoured Division.

To avoid detection and attack from the air, during the night of 4/5 August the KPA 13th Division moved out from Sangju, heading southeast toward the ROKA 1st Division sector and Taegu 40 miles away.

On 5 August, the KPA 13th Division's 21st Regiment waded neck-deep though the Naktong at Naktong-ni, followed that night by the 19th Regiment. Both units had to leave their heavy weapons and vehicles behind on the west bank. On the night of 6/7 August, the third regiment, the 23rd, accompanied by two artillery battalions, crossed the Naktong lower down on rafts.

In the north, between 6 and 8 August the KPA 1st Division crossed the Naktong into the ROKA 2nd Division's sector. Still at half strength, the division struck south toward Kunwi in the ROKA 6th Division's sector. A week after penetrating the South Korean defences, the KPA 13th Division met with the KPA 1st Division at Tabu-dong, a scant 15 miles north of Taegu.

To the west, after receiving 1,500 replacement troops at Kimch'ŏn, the 6,500-strong KPA 15th Division also started to move. The division's 45th Regiment struck east toward the Naktong, passing through Sonsan where they crossed the river. By first light on 8 August, the division's other two regiments, the 48th and 50th, had commenced crossing the Naktong between Andong and Waegwan. The division's support armour and vehicles also crossed. Once on the east bank, the division took hills 201 and 346, and continued east toward the mountains at Tabu-dong.

To the extreme south of the line on the boundary with the US 24th Division, on 8 August the unblooded KPA 10th Division arrived at Tŭksŏng-dong on the Naktong River, opposite the US 7th Cavalry Regiment and elements of the ROKA 17th Regiment. On the night of 11/12 August, the division's 2nd Battalion, 29th Regiment, waded across a much shallower Naktong near Hyongp'ung, where they entrenched on Hill 265 and the northern ridge of Hill 409. To the north, in the early hours of 12 August, the division's 25th Regiment crossed to the river's east bank. The 27th regiment was retained in reserve.

To the north of the US 1st Cavalry's boundary with the South Koreans, at 3 a.m. on the morning of 9 August, the 7th Regiment, KPA 3rd Division crossed the Naktong near Noch'ŏn. Half an hour later the division's other two regiments, the 8th and 9th, started to cross, but US 5th Cavalry Regiment artillery, mortar, machine-gun and small-arms fire ensured that very few North Koreans arrived on the east bank.

MEDAL OF HONOR RECIPIENT: KOREAN WAR

SEBILLE, Louis J.
Rank and organization: Major, U.S. Air Force, 67th Fighter-Bomber Squadron, 18th Fighter-Bomber Group, 5th Air Force.
Place and date: Near Hanchang [Hamch'ang], Korea, 5 August 1950.
Entered service at: Chicago, Ill.
Born: 21 November 1915, Harbor Beach. Mich.

CITATION: Maj. Sebille, distinguished himself by conspicuous gallantry and intrepidity at the risk of his life above and beyond the call of duty. During an attack on a camouflaged area containing a concentration of enemy troops, artillery, and armored vehicles, Maj. Sebille's F-51 aircraft was severely damaged by antiaircraft fire. Although fully cognizant of the short period he could remain airborne, he deliberately ignored the possibility of survival by abandoning the aircraft or by crash landing, and continued his attack against the enemy forces threatening the security of friendly ground troops. In his determination to inflict maximum damage upon the enemy, Maj. Sebille again exposed himself to the intense fire of enemy gun batteries and dived on the target to his death.

The superior leadership, daring, and selfless devotion to duty which he displayed in the execution of an extremely dangerous mission were an inspiration to both his subordinates and superiors and reflect the highest credit upon himself, the U.S. Air Force, and the armed forces of the United Nations.

(Center of Military History, United States Army)

At Eighth Army HQ in Taegu, early on 9 August, US 1st Cavalry Division commander, Major General Hobart Raymond 'Hap' Gay, began receiving signals about North Korean crossings into his sector south of Waegwan. Placing the 1st Battalion, 7th Cavalry Regiment (1/7th Cav) on one-hour standby, Gay received a briefing from the 5th Cavalry Regiment's acting intelligence officer (S-2), Lieutenant Harry A. Buckley, who had just arrived from his regiment's frontline positions south of Waegwan. The young officer reported: "Just prior to daylight this morning, I, with a small group of men from the I&R [Intelligence & Reconnaissance] Platoon, was on reconnaissance. Approximately 45 minutes prior to daylight, I observed enemy forces moving up the ridge line just northwest of Hill 268. The enemy were moving at

An American 105mm howitzer in action on the Kum River. (Photo US Army)

a dog trot in groups of four. Every fourth man carried an automatic weapon, either a light machine gun or a burp gun. I watched them until they had all disappeared into the brush on Hill 268. In my opinion, and I counted them carefully, the enemy was in strength of a reinforced battalion, approximately 750 men. General, I am not a very excitable person and I know what I saw, when I saw it, where I was when I saw it, and where the enemy was going."

Gay's response was immediate. Orders were issued to the commanding officer of 1/7th Cav, Lieutenant Colonel Peter D. Clainos, to take care of the North Koreans on Hill 268. Sitting on a vital line of communication, the strategic hill had to be taken and held. With five M-24 Chaffee tanks from A Company, 71st Tank Battalion, in support, Clainos moved his motorized force to his objective—better known as Triangulation Hill—three miles southeast of Waegwan.

At midday, the 61st FAB's 105mm howitzers laid down a bombardment onto the hilltop in preparation for the 1/7th Cav's attack. In the unbearable heat of the day, the Americans started to scale the hill, struggling to penetrate dense four-foot-high scrub. Many succumbed to heat exhaustion, and together with uncoordinated artillery support, the troops were beaten back down by elements of the 7th Regiment, KPA 3rd Division.

The following morning, a combined American air and artillery attack pounded and strafed the hill. At the same time, Gay ordered five tanks down the Waegwan road to engage the enemy from the northwest rear slopes. A short while later, Gay, who had arrived with his aide near the hill to talk to the battalion executive officer, was almost killed when an enemy mortar bomb exploded among the small group of American officers. Except for Gay and his aide, the others were all killed or wounded. Finding themselves hemmed in by overpowering American fire, North Korean resistance collapsed as those who still could fled the hilltop. By 4 p.m., the 1/7th Cav had taken the hill, and were engaged in clearing-up operations.

The American guns now swung to the west to cut off the retreating North Koreans, with white phosphorus ordnance from the 61st FAB killing 200 KPA troops in a nearby village. Leaving their 5th Cavalry comrades to finish securing Triangulation Hill, 1/7th Cav retired to resume their holding position as divisional reserve.

Intelligence gleaned from KPA prisoners confirmed that of the 1,000-strong KPA 7th regiment that had crossed the Naktong to Hill 268, more than 700 had become casualties. Elsewhere in the sector, other sister regiments of the KPA 3rd Division met the same fate, and by 12 August the division's strength had been reduced to a dysfunctional 2,500 men. During the fight for Triangulation Hill 1/7th Cav sustained 62 casualties, including 14 killed.

To the south, as part of an orchestrated attack to assist the KPA 3rd Division take Taegu, on the night of 11/12 August the 2nd Battalion, 29th Regiment, KPA 10th Division waded through the Naktong River near Hyŏngp'ung. Having attained their objective and establishing machine-gun emplacements on Hill 265, regimental sister 1st and 3rd battalions also crossed to occupy adjoining Hill 409. On the regiment's left flank, the KPA 25th Regiment arrived on the east bank at Tŭksŏng-dong, 14 miles southwest of Taegu.

At first light, several hundred KPA troops marched through Yong'po to Wich'ŏn-dong, where a firefight ensued with forward elements of H Company, 2nd Battalion, US 7th Cavalry Regiment (2/7th Cav). After overrunning American heavy machine-guns positions and a mortar observation post, the North Koreans were, however, checked by the 2/7th Cav supported by the 77th FAB and airstrikes. The North Koreans were pushed back to the Naktong where they bombshelled.

Undeterred, two days later—14 August—a 500-strong force from the KPA 10th Division, supported by artillery and tank fire, crossed the Naktong at the same point as previously. At around 9.20 a.m., the North Koreans encountered 2/th Cav positions only a mile to the east of the river. At 8 a.m., Clainos and his 1/7th Cav, held in reserve but already embussed in trucks, were ordered by Gay to lend support to the 2/7th Cav.

An American soldier fires an M1918A2 Browning Automatic Rifle (BAR). (Photo US Army)

On the west bank, North Korean troops were assembling in readiness for the crossing. As several barges started to ferry troops across, American aircraft bombed and strafed the North Koreans, while the 77th FAB fired 1,860 shells. Some KPA troops were only able to penetrate a mile and a half from the Naktong to Samuni-dong, where a withering curtain of combined rifle, machine-gun, mortar and artillery fire from the Americans stopped them dead in their tracks. By midday, the KPA attack had turned into a rout. Squashed against the Naktong trying to escape to the west bank, the North Koreans were sitting targets for American artillery and mortar fire and casualties were extremely heavy.

As the light began to fade, the US 7th Cavalry Regiment had neutralized the North Korean bridgehead. The KPA 10th Division's 25th and 27th regiments suffered debilitating casualty levels. It was later estimated that, of the 1,700 KPA troops that had crossed into the 7th Cavalry's sector on the east bank of the Naktong, 1,500 were killed. The Americans lost two killed.

CLASSIFICATION: SECRET

Date: 6 September 1950
Country: Korea
Subject: North Korean Military Activities

1. On 19 August the North Korean 8 Division was commanded by Major General O. Paek-yong. The division consists of three regiments and has a total strength of 5,000 men. The division is equipped with twenty-four 120mm guns [sic mortars], fifty-four 82mm guns [sic mortars], eighteen 45mm guns, four tanks, and an unspecified number of type SCR-300 radios captured from U.S. forces. The division is short of food, ammunition and medical supplies.
2. On 15 August two regiments of North Korean guerrilla troops led by North Korean Lt. Col. NA Yon-chol left Taejon to infiltrate Taegu and take it over by the end of August. The guerrillas are armed with rifles, and each company has about six mortars or pack howitzers. Each regiment has one signal platoon. Ten percent of the force are women.
3. In mid-August North Korean soldiers reported that the recent B-29 bombing of Waegwan hit a concentration of 40,000 volunteer army troops and inflicted heavy casualties (number unknown). The troops scattered and just regrouped north of the ROK 1st Division in mid-August.
   (Central Intelligence Agency Information Report FLO 630, CIA Library)

In distant Tokyo, commander of UN forces in Korea, General Douglas MacArthur, was growing increasingly concerned about the threat to Taegu. Should Taegu fall to the North Koreans, then Pusan would follow and the US Eighth Army pushed into the sea.

On 13 August, MacArthur summoned General George E. Stratemeyer, commanding general of the US Far East Air Force (FEAF), to his office to discuss the employment of the entire B-29 Superfortress force to carpet-bomb KPA enemy concentrations. With a reputation as a skilled military air tactician, Stratemeyer's command comprised the Fifth Air Force in occupied Japan, the Thirteenth Air Force in the Philippines, Twentieth Air Force in Okinawa, eighteen fighter and fighter-bomber groups, and one wing of Martin B-26 Marauders and Boeing B-29 Superfortresses. That same afternoon, the Fifth Air Force, commanded by General Earl E. Partridge, was informed that MacArthur had placed all available B-29s for ground-support operations in Korea on 15 August.

US President Harry S. Truman greets General Douglas MacArthur on Wake Island, 1950. (Photo US Army)

Commander of FEAF Bomber Command, Major General Emmett O'Donnell, expressed support for the proposed carpet-bombing of North Korean military concentrations, but required assurances that a positive outcome would be guaranteed. He was confident that effective saturation bombings with 500-pound bombs in a three-square-mile target area could be achieved with available aircraft. For optimum destruction, fragmentation bombs would have been employed, but there was not sufficient time to replace the general-purpose bombs with which the B-29s had already been loaded. O'Donnell stressed the need for essential prerequisites to ensure the success of any given raid: a cloud ceiling high enough to facilitate visual target identification, a clearly delineated flight path parallel to the frontline, a visible bombing-run line on the ground such as the Naktong River and, finally, confirmed intelligence that any given three-square-mile target area contained at least two North Korean divisions.

Despite being presented with a 27-square-mile target area by Walker, O'Donnell gave the go-ahead on being informed that the target held 40,000 KPA troops who were about to attack the US 1st Cavalry Division. However, low cloud over the Waegwan target area delated the operation to 16 August. Air force operational staff had divided the area into 12 equal-sized squares and aircrews cautioned that all bombs had to be dropped west of the Naktong River to avoid bombing American troops on the east bank.

Just before noon, the first squadron of B-29s arrived over the target area. Thirty minutes later, 98 of these heavy bombers, operating at between 5,000 and 10,000 feet, had dropped 3,084 500-pound and 150 1,000-pound bombs over the designated target. Not since the D-Day Normandy invasion in June 1944 had this magnitude of air support for ground forces been carried out.

Subsequent reconnaissance of the target area revealed an absence of North Korean troops and equipment. O'Donnell would recommend that no further carpet-bombing raids should be conducted unless the loss of ground to massed enemy advances was imminent. A disappointed Stratemeyer personally informed

Naktong River near Waegwan after US Air Force B-29s conducted a mass strike in August 1950. (Photo US Army)

MacArthur that his air-support capabilities were best utilized by the employment of fighter-bombers and carrier-borne dive-bombers. The B-29s would resume with interdiction raids in North Korea and Task Force 77 brought back to support Walker's ground forces.

While regiments of the US 1st Cavalry Division were fighting to stem attacks on Tŭksŏng-dong and Yong'po, to the north of Waegwan elements of the KPA 3rd Division fell on Hill 303, the first hilly terrain north of the town. The hill feature commanded the extreme right flank of the US Eighth Army, overlooking a north–south road along the Naktong River's east bank and controlling the main Seoul–Pusan rail line. At the time, G Company of the US 5th Cavalry Regiment held Hill 303.

In the early hours of 14 August, North Korean troops crossed the Naktong over an underwater bridge six miles north of Waegwan, immediately attacking ROKA 13th Regiment positions on high ground above the US/ROKA armies' boundary. But instead of striking east, the regimental-strength KPA force veered south toward Hill 303. By noon, the North Koreans had started to engage G Company with small-arms fire.

Just before first light on 15 August, the Americans on Hill 303 spotted around 50 KPA troops and two T-34 tanks advancing down the road along the base of the hill which rose some 950 feet above the road. Behind this column, another was engaging F Company with small-arms fire. Fearing envelopment, F Company retired southward. By 8.30 a.m., G Company and a mortar platoon from H Company had been isolated by the North Koreans. In an attempt to relieve their encircled comrades, B Company, 5th Cavalry, with tank support, was repelled by heavy enemy fire.

The next day, B Company with tank support was again driven back by an estimated 700 North Koreans now holding the hill. Throughout the day, the 61st FAB and three howitzers from B Battery, 82nd FAB, pounded North Korean positions of the hill. Under cover of darkness, G Company were able to vacate their positions of the hill.

Early on 17 August, an American force comprising 1st and 2nd battalions, US 5th Cavalry Regiment, supported by elements of the 70th Tank Battalion (attached to the US 1st Cavalry Division and equipped with M46 Patton and M4A3E8 Sherman tanks) launched an attack on Hill 303. However, heavy mortar fire from the North Koreans above stalled their advance on the outskirts of Waegwan.

American artillery then laid down a heavy barrage on the hill, the 61st FAB alone firing 1,159 shells from its 105mm howitzers. Following a request from divisional HQ at 11.30 a.m. for an airstrike on the hill, at 2 p.m. US aircraft bombed (including napalm), rocketed and strafed the already crippled North Koreans into oblivion. At 3.30 p.m., E and F companies successfully scaled the hill, taking only an hour to secure their position. Around 200 enemy bodies, many badly mutilated, were discovered. It was estimated that the North Koreans on Hill 303 suffered 500 casualties.

DISTINGUISHED SERVICE CROSS

CARDOZA, Howard W.

Citation:
The President of the United States takes pleasure in presenting the Distinguished Service Cross to Howard W. Cardoza (o-1177318), First Lieutenant (Armor), U.S. Army, for extraordinary heroism in connection with military operations against an armed enemy of the United Nations while serving with Headquarters and Service Company, 70th Tank Battalion (Heavy), attached to the 1st Cavalry Division. First Lieutenant Cardoza distinguished himself by extraordinary heroism in action against enemy aggressor forces at Waegwan, Korea, on 16 August 1950.

Lieutenant Cardoza's tank platoon was operating in direct support of the infantry whose mission was to take a hill just outside of Waegwan. The enemy, well entrenched on the hill, was delivering intense small-arms, mortar, and artillery fire. Lieutenant Cardoza moved his tank forward to the infantry positions in order to place fire on the enemy. Then, with total disregard for his personal safety, he crawled out of the tank onto the rear deck to direct the fire of his platoon. Firing the .50-caliber machine-gun, which was mounted on the turret, Lieutenant Cardoza in this manner pointed out the enemy targets to his gunners. During this action an enemy shell exploded next to Lieutenant Cardoza's tank seriously wounding him in the head, legs and arm. Although his left arm was useless, he continued to fire the .50-caliber machine-gun with one arm until he collapsed from loss of blood. It was only because of the devastating tank fire directed by Lieutenant Cardoza on the enemy that the infantry was able to continue on and accomplish its mission.

Headquarters, Eighth U.S. Army, Korea: General Orders No. 99 (October 5, 1950)
Home Town: Mercer, Pennsylvania
(1st Cavalry Division Association)

Tragically, the cavalrymen would stumble across a far more gruesome and shocking sight: 26 members of the H Company mortar team, their hands bound behind their backs with wire, brutally murdered by their communist captors. A 5th Cavalry Regiment Intelligence and Reconnaissance officer attending the scene reported: "The boys lay packed tightly, shoulder to shoulder, lying on their sides, curled like babies sleeping in the sun. Their feet, bloodied and bare, from

US medical corpsmen attend to the walking wounded. (Photo US Army)

walking on the rocks, stuck out stiffly. All had hands tied behind their backs, some with cord, others with regular issue army communication wire. Only a few of the hands were clenched.'*

Details gleaned from survivor Private Roy Manring and two KPA prisoners, helped the division to piece together the sequence of events that culminated in the atrocity, perpetrated by soldiers who treated international conventions or protocol applicable to prisoners of war with total disdain. In a dire case of mistaken identity that would have grim consequences, early on 15 August the troops of H Company heavy mortar platoon on Hill 303 mistook KPA soldiers approaching them up the slope to be a party of ROKA troops sent by the officer commanding G Company, 5th Cavalry, to reinforce their position. The North Koreans, later thought to have been from the 4th Company, 2nd Battalion, 206th Mechanized Infantry Regiment of the KPA 105th Armoured Division, strolled

---

* Roy E. Appleman, 'South to the Naktong, North to the Yalu: June–November 1950'

An American anti-tank gun near Waegwan. (Photo US Army)

up to the American foxholes unchallenged. Now prisoners of the KPA, the hapless Americans had their shoes and certain items of clothing removed and their hands crudely tied behind their backs. During their first night in captivity, the Americans were treated to cigarettes and given fruit and water. The North Koreans had intended to take their captives back across the Naktong, but concentrated American fire thwarted their plans. The prisoners spent an uneventful day on 16 August, listening to American attacks on the hill. That night five of their number were taken away to an unknown fate.

Early the following morning, US troops came so close that the North Koreans guarding the American prisoners exchanged fire with the assailants. Around midday, the nervous North Koreans placed the prisoners in a small gulley under the care of a few guards. The American artillery bombardment and airstrikes now took place, placing the North Koreans in an untenable situation. A North Korean officer then gave the H Company troops the chilling news that they had now become a liability and would be shot.

What transpired next remains uncertain as survivors recalled two versions of the massacre. According to some, the whole company of 50 North Koreans opened fire with PPSh41 'burp' guns, while others contend that some 14 North Koreans ran up to the gulley before firing into the huddled Americans. The slaughter of prisoners of war on Hill 303 took place in spite of orders from KPA Commander-in-Chief, Kim Chaek, and Kang Kon, Commanding General Staff, of the army general headquarters. MacArthur was outraged, and included in a strongly worded message on a leaflet airdrop over North Korea, he warned: "Inertia on your part and on the part of your senior field commanders in the discharge of this grave and universally recognized command responsibility may only be construed as a condonation and encouragement of such outrage, for which if not promptly corrected I shall hold you and your commanders criminally accountable under the rules and precedents of war."[*]

By mid-August, pressure from the KPA 15th, 13th and 1st divisions continued to mount on Major General Paik Sun Yup's ROKA 1st Division. Not for the first time, US military intelligence had erred in declaring that the main North Korean offensive would be centred on Waegwan, when in fact the main thrust came from the north. While elements of the ROKA 13th Regiment held their positions along a stretch of the Naktong to the immediate north of Waegwan, the ROKA 12th and 11th regiments were battling it out with the KPA in the mountainous terrain of Suam-san and Yuhak-san, four to six miles east of the Naktong.

Refugees fleeing the advancing North Koreans more than doubled Taegu's civilian population to 700,000 and, on 16 August, 750 South Korean police were positioned on the city's outskirts as an early warning precaution. Two days later, seven KPA artillery shells fell in the city, prompting South Korean President Syngman Rhee to evacuate his provincial government to Pusan. This sparked the commencement of a mass evacuation by the city's residents, which also had a negative impact on the morale of troops garrisoned in Taegu. The Eighth Army acted immediately to stem the civilian evacuation. Following a third and final shelling of the city by North Korean artillery, a further six battalions of South Korean police were deployed to guard key road and rail lines of communication.

Early on the afternoon of 17 August, Walker ordered the 27th Regiment 'Wolfhounds', US 25th Division, to move its tactical HQ three miles north of Taegu to a point across the Kumho River on the Tabu-dong–Sangju road, dubbed 'the Bowling Alley' by the Americans. Having just returned from the US 24th Division sector in the Naktong Bulge, commanding officer Colonel John H. 'Iron Mike' Michaelis's task was clear: keep the North Koreans from reaching Taegu.

---

[*] Ibid

DRAFT
REPORT OF A US AIR FORCE OFFICER—FORMERLY PRISONER IN NORTH KOREA

I was flying F-51s [Mustangs] on August 17th [1950], and we were strafing enemy positions about 40 miles inside enemy territory. My cooling system was shot out and I didn't quite make it back to friendly territory. I belly landed about 5 miles inside the front lines, and the area that I bellied into was full of North Korean troops. This same area was the area that was later bombed to hell by the B-29s [Superfortress] when the UN forces started their offensive in September.

Immediately after getting out the airplane, the field was surrounded and they continued to fire out over my head at the wreckage and I crawled a couple of hundred yards away from the scene of the accident before I was finally captured.

I was taken into the hills about 3 to 5 miles from the scene of the accident, and they held me there for 2 days and nights. They kept me pretty well tied up and guarded during this time. They wired my hands and feet together with wire and actually had me tied to a tree during the hours of darkness. In daylight they would untie me, but I was pretty well guarded, and my chances of escaping at that time were, you might say nil.

I underwent quite a bit of interrogation during this period of time. They expected me to know the position of all our ground force troops and our artillery around the city of Taegu. They had high hopes of taking the city of Taegu and ending the war within a couple of weeks. Remember that at this time we were holding a very small piece of ground beginning at Taegu, on down along the Nantong River down to the Pusan beach head.

After two days and night sin the hills they decided to take us to Seoul. After 2 or 3 nights of marching we ran into a group of 35 American prisoners and 8 more South Korean prisoners. We arrived in Seoul on the 28th of August.

On the night of September 20th, on the spur of the moment ... they told us we were all going to be taken to Pyongyang, the North Korean capital. At this time we had 376 prisoners. I was the only Air Force man in the group—all the rest of them were army prisoners. During the 19 days march from Seoul to Pyongyang, 80 of our prisoners died or were killed. On the morning of October 8th, this flight of F-80s [Shooting Star] spotted us and gave us a working over and 15 of the 50 men in the group were killed and several badly wounded. The rest of the men died of dysentery ... our biggest enemy.

(Central Intelligence Agency Library)

The 1st Battalion, 27th Regiment (1/27th), a platoon of the Heavy Mortar Company and the 8th FAB—less B Battery—provided the vanguard, arriving at the ROKA 1st Division HQ at Ch'ilgok later that day. By last light the whole 27th Regiment was in place, supported by C Company from the 73rd Tank Battalion. With the sound of enemy artillery fire ever closer, Walker also moved the 37th FAB—less A Battery—to bolster the 8th FAB's firepower north of his HQ. Confronting the UN forces were three KPA divisions: 13th (Choi Yong Chin), 1st (Hong Rim) and 15th (Paik Son Choi).

After battling the ROKA 11th and 12th regiments for several days in the Yuhaksan area, by 18 August the KPA 13th Division had penetrated the Tabu-dong corridor to the south. Despite having sustained an estimated 1,500 casualties, the KPA 13th Division consolidated its position to the west of the Tabu-dong road just north of the town, a short 13 miles from an edgy Taegu. Intelligence reported the presence of 13 T-34 tanks from the KPA 105th Armoured Division in the division.

On the KPA 13th Division's right flank, the KPA 15th Division was dug in on Yuhaksan. However, this would be a transient deployment, as by 20 August the division

M2 90mm anti-aircraft guns of the ROKA 1st Division fire on North Korean positions north of Taegu. (Photo US Army)

had been moved eastward where the KPA 8th Division had stalled in the Yŏngch'ŏn sector. At the same time, the KPA 1st Division had struck south through Kunwi to position themselves on the KPA 13th Division's left flank in the Tabu-dong area. The North Koreans were poised to fall on Taegu. Once taken, Pusan would be the remaining objective to rid the peninsula of foreign forces.

On 18 August, Walker launched a pre-emptive strike against the assembling North Koreans. Supported by M26 Pershing tanks and two batteries of howitzers, the 27th Regiment would strike north along the main road, trucking their way to the narrow, tree-lined mountain valley that was the Bowling Alley. Two ROKA regiments would simultaneously attack and take the village of Sokch'ŏk to the east of the 27th and four miles north of Tabu-dong.

Following effective tactical airstrikes by F-51 Mustang fighters from southern Japan, the 1/27th and 2/27th crossed the line of departure at 3.30 p.m. However, after advancing 3,000 yards, during which only light KPA resistance was encountered, the RCT commander called a halt at 5.30 p.m. as the ROKA units on his flanks were failing to match his pace. While 1/27th and 2/27th established all-round defences for the night straddling the road at Kuhmwa-dong, the 3/27th, supported by C Company, 65th Engineer Battalion, dug in about 3,000 yards south of the main line of resistance (MLR). The attack would resume at first light if the ROKA units had arrived at the night bivouac and were able to secure the Americans' flanks.

That night—18/19 August—the North Koreans attacked the 1/27th and 3/27th positions. The US 25th Division's war records relate the events of that night: "Preceded by tank and artillery fire, enemy launched attack with estimated battalion. At approximately 182000 August; infantry in carriers or trucks was preceded by tanks which delivered fire throughout the area. 8th FA Battalions delivered fire on attacking elements, temporarily halting advance. Enemy continued attack with infantry until approximately 21.30, attempting to penetrate 1st and 2d Battalion positions astride road. Three enemy tanks closed to vicinity of forward positions supporting infantry; these were destroyed by close in artillery fire and 3.5 bazooka fire from Company F. Suffering from losses inflicted by our forces, enemy withdrew ... At 190230, undetermined number of enemy again probed 2d Battalion positions employing two tanks in support. This attack dispersed by artillery, mortar and small arms fire."[*]

At first light on 19 August, fresh attacks by ROKA 11th and 13th regiments failed to secure the 27th's flanks, despite having made some gains. Walker moved the ROKA 10th Regiment forward to fill the gap between the ROKA 1st and 6th divisions. At 4 p.m. the general ordered the 3rd Battalion, 23rd Regiment (3/23rd) to provide perimeter defence for the 8th and 37th FAB positions eight miles north of his HQ.

---

[*] 25th Infantry Division History, August 1950, Tropic Lightning in Korea, NARA

Sunday 20 August was a day of relative quiet on the Taegu front. General Partridge evacuated most of his Fifth Air Force personnel from Taegu, while the JOC was moved to Pusan. However, the new forward line held. In a visit later that day, Walker declared that Taegu "certainly is saved." The US 27th Regiment war records reflect: "Battalions continued improvement of positions on 20 August emplacing trip flares, anti-tank and antipersonnel mines fields. Tactical air strikes and artillery fires continued to wreak havoc on enemy troop concentrations and artillery positions. Damage caused by air and artillery could not be immediately determined but later reports by PWs [prisoners of war] and observers indicated excellent results; this action probably prevented enemy from accomplishing build-up of forces generally north of positions. Main activity of enemy was mortar and artillery fire directed over entire RCT zone."*

The North Koreans came back during the night of 20/21 August, attacking 1/27th and 2/27th forward positions at 9.30 p.m. with tanks and self-propelled guns. Retaliating with mortar and artillery fire, the UN troops only opened fire with small arms when the North Koreans were within easy shooting distance. Tanks of C Company, 73rd Tank Battalion joined the firefight, engaging the North Korean T-34s at close range. The enemy broke off their attack at midnight.

At 7.45 a.m. on 21 August, elements of B and G companies, with a section of tanks in support, launched a limited-objective attack north along the road to determine enemy losses. Forced to retire after enemy self-propelled gun fire halted the patrol's expedition after 1,500 yards, the troops reported discovering an abandoned KPA 37mm anti-tank gun, its crew dead, five disabled T-34 tanks which they destroyed with thermite grenades, two self-propelled guns, a 120mm mortar and 20 dead North Korean troops.

That night, 27th Regiment forward positions came under KPA artillery fire, followed around midnight by a large attack on ROKA and American positions by elements of the KPA 13th Division. To the west of the road, C Company reported the sound of approaching tanks. An illuminating shell confirmed that a column of 19 KPA vehicles were closing in at a brisk pace, tanks and self-propelled guns firing as they came.

An intense firefight ensued for five hours. In support of the 2/27th, B Battery of the 8th FAB alone fired 1,660 shells, the 4.2-inch and 81mm mortar platoon fired 900 and 1,200 bombs respectively, while F Company fired 385 60mm mortar bombs. An American Pershing knocked out the leading KPA T-34 tank from only 125 yards, as an F Company 3.5-inch bazooka team disabled a self-propelled gun that was positioned third in the column. Trapped and disabled by a bazooka rocket, the North Korean tank caught in between was abandoned by its crew. Artillery and tank fire accounted

---

* Ibid

RESTRICTED
HEADQUARTERS 25TH INFANTRY DIVISION

APO 25
17 August 1950
Subject: Abandonment of U.S. Army Equipment

1. It has come to the attention of this headquarters that elements of this division and attached units are needlessly abandoning U.S. Army equipment. This has occurred during normal displacements and movements not subject to enemy fire or threat.
2. The leaving of unguarded supplies or equipment behind during an advance is a practice which cannot be tolerated. The enemy who opposes us frequently operates behind our lines in civilian dress. By leaving supplies behind or unguarded, we are facilitating his problem of supply, increasing the chances for attack on the rear of our lines, and generally endangering the success of our mission in Korea.
3. The dangers inherent in the abandonment or loss of equipment and supplies will immediately be brought to the attention of all personnel of your unit. Continuing vigorous supervision will be exercised by all officers and non-commissioned officers to instil the discipline necessary to eliminate any further loss or abandonment of supplies and equipment.
4. Prior to departure from an area the unit commander will cause an inspection to be made to ensure that no usable supplies, or items of equipment, have been left behind. In instances where the tactical situation precludes the possibility of removal of supplies or equipment, they will be destroyed by any means available.

By Command of Major General Kean
(Record Group 407: Army-AG Command Reports, 1949-54, NARA)

for a further seven enemy T-34s, another three self-propelled guns and a miscellany of trucks and personnel carriers. An estimated 1,300 North Koreans became casualties during that night's engagement. The column was completely destroyed.

Although Walker was now considerably more confident of retaining Taegu, the bolstering of UN defences continued unabated. Replacing 3/23rd, the 2/23rd maintained

The Soviet-made 37mm air defence gun M1939 (61-K) used extensively by the North Koreans during the conflict.

the infantry role of protecting their artillery from KPA attack. The North Koreans, meanwhile, persisted with irregular acts of attrition.

At 5 p.m. on 22 August, reports were received that North Korean positions on high ground east of the road had opened fire with mortars, self-propelled guns and small-arms fire on the MSR. It had transpired that elements of a KPA infantry regiment had penetrated ROKA defences and taken commanding positions of the main road: "Enemy was engaged by Headquarters, Medical and Artillery personnel. 3d Battalion, 23d Infantry also engaged enemy by fire and offensive action. Enemy had infiltrated through ROK positions east of own forces, assembled and established positions dominating MSR. Own forces engaged enemy with artillery, mortars, and small arms and tank fire forcing enemy off the high ground ... Several effective air strikes were made on enemy located along ridge and in valley rear of ridge; these strikes included Air Force, Navy and Australian fighter-bombers strafing and rocketing positions. A B-26 bomber strike, using 44,000 pounds of bombs added the final blow.""*

---

*   Ibid

US 25th Division artillery softens up enemy positions.

By the end of 24 August, intelligence and reconnaissance patrols as well as infantry combat units in the 23rd Regiment sector estimated that no more than 200 KPA troops remained to their front. That night the North Koreans conducted another of their perfunctory night raids but were repelled.

In the period from 17 to 25 August, combined UN air and ground forces accounted for three KPA tanks and six self-propelled guns, while inflicting 3,000 casualties.

Through the night of 24 August until 3.45 a.m. the next day, all units in the Taegu sector were relieved. The US 25th Division RCT, the 27th, returned to division in Masan to the south. The perimeter in the Taegu sector held and Walker's Eighth Army headquarters remained secure, if badly shaken.

4. EASTERN CORRIDOR

Situated at the mouth of the Hyŏngsan'gang River where it flows into the Sea of Japan on the South Korean east coast, the port city of P'ohang was of vital strategic importance to both the North Koreans and the beleaguered UN forces.

Along the east–west axis of the Pusan defensive perimeter, North Korean operations in the central, mountainous region fell under the control of the KPA II Corps. Headquartered at Hwach'on, the corps had a new commander in the person of Lieutenant General Kim Mu Chong, the previous incumbent, Lieutenant General Kim Kwang Hypo having been relieved of his post on 10 July after being deemed inefficient.

Earlier in the month, the North Korean high command had redesignated the KPA 7th Division the 12th and formed a new 7th Division. Immediately thereafter, the KPA 12th Division was deployed in two parts: southeast on Chech'ŏn and south on Ch'ungju.

To the south, in the perimeter line held by the ROKA I and II corps, the ROKA 8th Division had recently arrived from the coast, tasked with defending the Tanyang corridor. Having taken Ch'ungju and Chech'ŏn, the KPA 12th Division converged at Tanyang where it blocked the ROKA 8th Division on its march to Ch'ungju. At this stage the South Koreans appeared to lose cohesive command control when the decision was taken not to engage the KPA forces and push through to Ch'ungju. On the premise that his troops were exhausted, the division commander elected to retire to Yŏngch'ŏn, and from there move west to Taegu. Exasperated American KMAG advisors on the ground discovered that the division had splintered, finding elements at Yŏngch'ŏn, P'ohang and even as far away as Taegu. Communications re-established, ROKA army HQ issued fresh orders for the regroup to be railed back to positions on the upper Han River to defend the Yongju–Andong corridor. At Taegu, Walker was satisfied with deployments by 10 July along the Han-Naktong watershed in the centre, where commanding high ground secured the Tanyang and Mun'gyong mountain passes that accessed the south.

Spearheading the main North Korean offensive down the eastern flank, on 14 July the KPA 12th Division took the river crossing at Tanyang, before engaging the ROKA 8th Division for possession of the Tanyang Pass northwest of Yongju. Facing certain envelopment at the pass, the South Koreans were compelled to withdraw, allowing the KPA forces to push on to the Taebaek mountain passes at the head of the upper Naktong River valley.

Commander of the US Eighth Army, Lieutenant General Walton H. Walker, left, in discussion with the US 24th Division commander, Major General William F. Dean. (Photo US NARA)

With the inhospitable Taebaek Mountains forming a natural barrier from the fighting to the west, the KPA 5th Division and KPA 766th Independent Unit (766th IU) had marched virtually unchallenged south along the east coast. At Kanggu-dong, the 11th Regiment, KPA 5th Division (11/5th), undertook an exhausting 175-mile forced march inland to Ch'unyang, where a bitter firefight ensued with retiring elements of the ROKA 8th Division. The action deflected the North Koreans back to the east where, on 10 July, they had rejoined the main body of the division at Ulchin on the coast. Up to this point, the coastal expedition had cost the division 1,800 soldiers. At this juncture, the 766th IU infiltrated westward in small groups from Ulchin to conduct guerrilla-type sabotage operations against UNC lines of communication between Taegu and Pusan.

Curiously, the KPA 5th Division commander failed to exploit his strong position. While apparently dithering to prioritize his options, from 10 July the 23rd

Regiment, ROKA 3rd Division (23/3rd), attacked his forces from the south along a 20-mile coastal belt in between Ulchin and P'yŏnghae-ri. For the rest of the month, the antagonists battled hard for possession of the coastal road from Yŏngdŏk to P'ohang. Warships bombarded KPA 5th Division coastal concentrations, while Lockheed F-80 Shooting Star jets of the redesignated 35th Fighter-Bomber Squadron stationed at Yŏnil Airfield just to the south of P'ohang, strafed and bombed the North Koreans.

Commanded by the indomitable Colonel Kim 'Tiger Kim' Chong Won, the ROKA 23/3rd now received reinforcements in the form of 1,500 South Korean troops from the ROKA 1st and Yŏngdŭngp'o battalions. Against a determined foe and blighted by desertions, however, the ROKA 23/3rd was inexorably forced back to Yŏngdŏk where, on 12 July, Brigadier General Lee Chu Sik took over command of the ROKA 3rd Division.

'NEW' RUSSIAN JEEPS TAKEN IN KOREA

A special despatch to Reuters by Walter Simmons, "Chicago Tribune" correspondent, says that 20 North Korean jeeps captured north of Chongju yesterday, were new Russian models, none with more than 500 miles on its speedometer. They had apparently been in service less than a week. A Russian lorry captured in the same area had 501 miles on its speedometer. Planes with Red Star markings seen recently over South Korea are believed to be newly delivered Russian craft rushed into service before there was time to paint North Korean insignia on them.

Weapons Discarded
Meanwhile, although no announcement has been made, the United States obviously faces the task of rearming the South Korean army. Tens of thousands of weapons were thrown away in the hysterical retreat. Most of the South Koreans' artillery and transportation were also lost. Originally, the United States gave the Koreans about 150,000 rifles of various types. Some of them were used to arm the 50,000-man police force. The police—still armed—have fled by the thousands and always ahead of everyone else.

About half of the estimated tanks given to the enemy by the Soviets are believed destroyed. The Russians must now provide replacements.
Coventry Evening Telegraph, Wednesday, 12 July 1950

My mid-July, the KPA 5th Division had seized P'yŏnghae-ri, 22 miles north of Yŏngdŏk and only 50 miles from their objective, the strategic port city of P'ohang. In a desperate attempt to stop the North Korean war machine in its relentless march southward to P'ohang, the ROKA 3rd Division, assisted by KMAG advisers Captain Harold Slater and Captain John Airsman, hurriedly established a fire-control centre south of Yŏngdŏk. From here, airstrikes, naval shelling and fire from the division's four batteries of 75mm pack howitzers and 105mm howitzers would be coordinated. KMAG advisor to the ROKA 3rd Division, Lieutenant Colonel Rollins S. Emmerich, despite incessant encouraging and cajoling of the ROKA 23/3rd, responded to an inquiry from Walker's Eighth Army HQ: "Situation deplorable, things are popping, trying to get something established across the front, 75% of the 23d ROKA Regiment is on the road moving south. Advisers threatening and shooting in the air trying to get them assembled, Commanding General forming a straggler line. If straggler line is successful we may be able to reorganize and re-establish the line. If this fails I am afraid that the whole thing will develop in complete disintegration. The Advisory Group needs food other than Korean or C rations and needs rest."[*]

On 17 July, the North Koreans took Yŏngdŏk, heralding the onset of three weeks of bitter fighting, punctuated by the vacillating fortunes of the opposing forces as first one then the other regained control of a desolate stretch of real estate on the southern outskirts of the town. The very next day, the UN forces retaliated with airstrikes at dawn, followed by a star-shell signal from the American light cruiser USS *Juneau* for the commencement of the shelling of immediate coastal enemy positions as well as interdiction fire to the North Korean rear. For the KPA 5th Division, although suffering significant losses, it was a temporary setback. Consolidating three miles along the road north of Yŏngdŏk, 24 hours later the North Koreans seized Yŏngdŏk once more.

A week earlier, Emmerich had travelled to Yŏnil Airfield (USAF Field K-3) five miles south of P'ohang, where he entered into urgent discussions with Colonel Robert W. Witty, commander of the US 35th Fighter Interceptor Group and 6131st Tactical Support Wing. The meeting was also attended by generals Walker and Partridge who had flown in from Taegu, and commander of the US 25th Division, General Kean. Emmerich expressed his growing concern that elements of the KPA 12th Division were infiltrating the ROKA line between the 3rd and Capital divisions, thereby presenting an immediate threat to the security of the airfield, and from there, P'ohang. Walker issued orders for the ROKA 3rd Division to retake and hold Yŏngdŏk at all costs, an imperative not well received by the South Koreans.

---

[*]   Roy E. Appleman, 'South to the Naktong, North to the Yalu, June-November 1950'

The US Navy battleship USS *Missouri* (BB-63) at anchor off the Korean east coast. The other ship is a British destroyer. (Photo US Navy)

With the added naval firepower from the American destroyers *Higbee, Mansfield, DeHaven* and *Swenson,* and the British cruiser HMS *Belfast,* fire from the naval vessels, artillery, mortars and fighter-bombers allowed the South Koreans to re-occupy Yŏngdŏk. The South Koreans suffered heavy casualties, but their victory was hollow: that night the KPA drove them out of the town again. Once more the North Koreans took unimaginable heavy air, sea and ground fire from the UN forces. Attempts to execute enveloping moves through the mountains to the west were met with the same punishment.

At this time, the 1st Battalion, US 7th Cavalry (1/7th Cav), commanded by Lieutenant Colonel Peter D. Clainos, was the third in a succession of American battalions to provide a block behind ROKA forces on the Yŏngdŏk–P'ohang coastal road. From its commanding position on Hill 181 (Round Top), C Company from 1/7th Cav looked on as the opposing Korean forces battled each other immediately to the south of Yŏngdŏk. On 24 July, the 21st Infantry Regiment, US 24th Division, took over from the 7th Cavalry.

To the south of Yŏngdŏk, the KPA 5th Division tenaciously and desperately clung on to two hills. At 8.30 a.m. on 27 July, another massive air, ground and sea barrage precipitated a bloody battle for Yŏngdŏk that would last until 2 August when the ROKA 3rd Division retook the town, pressing their counterattack north beyond Yŏngdŏk. KPA 5th Division casualties in the fortnight-long fight for Yŏngdŏk were estimated at 40 percent of its combat strength.

During this period, there were similar actions in the central mountains as the ROKA 8th Division stood in the way of the KPA 12th Division from crossing the Naktong River at Andong, from where the North Koreans planned to launch a flanking attack on P'ohang. From 21 July to the end of the month, some of the bloodiest fighting of the early stages of the Korean War took place between the two opposing divisions on the Yongju–Andong road. As the KPA 5th Division licked its wounds north of Yŏngdŏk, a frustrated KPA II Corps HQ ordered its 12th Division to seize P'ohang by 26 July. However, corps commander Lieutenant General Kim Mu Chong, unaware of the heavy fighting in the central mountains, would not have been cognizant of the near impossible task that he was demanding of his 12th Division.

To achieve this objective, the KPA 12th Division was forced to move in daylight hours, alien to KPA tactics throughout the theatre as it made them extremely vulnerable to air attacks. Undaunted, and despite daily harassment from UN aircraft and resistance from the South Koreans, on 1 August the KPA division captured Andong, and with it, the strategic Naktong River crossing by the town. But the division was haemorrhaging: more than a

The USS *Wisconsin* bombards the Korean coast. (Photo US Navy)

thousand casualties, the division's 2nd artillery battalion had used up all its ammunition and had returned to Tanyang with their guns, and only 19 of the division's original 30 T-34 tanks were serviceable. As a consequence, the KPA's advantage could not be exploited as the division required several days at the beginning of August to recoup and take stock.

General Walker clearly understood the dangers inherent in undervaluing the importance of P'ohang as a safe harbour to UN forces, even though the port of Pusan was the current—and only— logistical receiver of UN forces and supplies on the peninsula. Of greater concern to the US Eighth Army and ROKA commander was the highly important strategic position of P'ohang as a nexus for naturally occurring east–west and north–south corridors, yielding several key access routes into the North Koreans' main objective: Pusan. The 50-airmile-long road and rail MSR followed a valley corridor between Taegu and P'ohang. The only other such route to the east coast lay 225 miles to the north: the Seoul–Wonsan corridor.

At about midpoint along the route sits the town of Yŏngch'ŏn, a junction for the only north–south route between Taegu and P'ohang. It straddles the only passable road through the mountains from Andong to the north. The town of An'gang-ni is also situated on the Taegu corridor, some 12 miles west of P'ohang. To the north, Kigye nestles in the foothills of the Pihak mountain range at the start of a north–south valley corridor that passes through An'gang-ni and on to the rail and road hub at Kyongju to the south. From here, Pusan is 60 airmiles south. For Walker, the Taegu–Yŏngch'ŏn–An'gang-ni–Kyongju–Pusan corridors had to remain in the control of UN forces, fundamental in the prevention of the whole Korean peninsula from turning red.

However, the North Koreans were of the same mind, perceiving control of the eastern corridors and P'ohang as the prerequisite for the taking of Pusan. On the left flank of the sector, the ROKA 6th and 8th divisions, II Corps, were confronted by the advancing KPA 8th Division along the Ŭisŏng road toward Yŏngch'ŏn. In the ROKA I Corps sector, the KPA 12th Division penetrated the mountains to the southeast of Andong in a headlong march on P'ohang, while the KPA 766th IU left the coastal road in a southwesterly direction for the Kigye and An'gang-ni objectives. Also jumping off from Yŏngdŏk, the bulk of the KPA 5th Division moved directly south along the coastal road, with selected infantry units from the division striking inland to envelope the ROKA 3rd Division.

On 9 August, the ROKA 8th Division was successful at Ŭisŏng in blocking the KPA 8th Division from reaching the Taegu–P'ohang lateral corridor, engaging the North Koreans' 2nd and 3rd regiments, the latter suffering 700 casualties. At a bridge in a steep-sided section of the road, two KPA T-34 tanks detonated ROKA-planted anti-tank landmines on the road verges. As another T-34 and a 76mm self-propelled gun approached, a wing of F-51 Mustangs swept in, rocketing and napalm-bombing the trapped KPA armour and destroying them all. The crippled KPA 8th Division was forced to halt to await reinforcements.

<u>SECRET</u>
CIA Analysis of the Korean War Overview: 1950-07-28

SOVIET/SATELLITE INTENTIONS

As the USSR and its Satellites continued to talk loudly of "peace" and the warlike intentions of the Western "imperialists," there was no slackening of reports that the USSR itself was preparing to initiate further aggressive moves around the Soviet perimeter. Although possessing the capability to move militarily in a number of places with little advance warning, with the possible exception of continued preparations for an attack on Taiwan, the USSR has not yet given any firm indication of its intention to expand the Korean conflict and increase the risk of global warfare involving the Soviet Union. Meanwhile, Soviet diplomatic activity was aimed primarily at South Asia and the Soviet Far East.

Korean support

Although there has been no evidence of troop movements from Manchuria into northern Korea since the outbreak of hostilities, North Korean forces may soon be reinforced by Korean veterans of the Chinese Communist Army. Within the next three weeks, North Korean forces will probably have made the maximum advance possible with the troops currently available in Korea. If the USSR desires a quick victory before UN forces are further reinforced, it will have to call upon additional, experienced troops for use in Korea.

Although the North Koreans may have committed practically all their available organized and trained units merely to achieve a quick victory regardless of the risk, it seems more probable that the Northern Command has been assured of reinforcements. Such reinforcements would at the minimum consist of the 40–50,000 Koreans believed to be available in Manchuria and would be used to replace the heavy casualties resulting from the rapid North Korean advance, to cover the exposed flanks and rear, and, if necessary, to provide momentum for the final push against reinforced UN troops. The USSR could use these "Korean" reinforcements with little danger of political repercussions. There is at present no indication, however, as to whether the USSR will risk the political disadvantages involved in committing non-Korean reinforcements should such a step become necessary.

(Central Intelligence Agency declassified archives)

At the same time, the depleted KPA 12th Division, now without the field pieces of its 2nd Battalion, Artillery Regiment, crossed the upper Naktong River before infiltrating the mountains. In response, the ROKA Capital Division was ordered to link up with the ROKA 3rd Division on the former's right flank to counteract the enemy threat in the so-called 'guerrilla area' in the mountains northwest of P'ohang.

On 9 August, and having just arrived from Taegu, the 1st and 2nd battalions, ROKA 25th Regiment were ordered to attack north of Kigye. However, the South Koreans only marched a short distance before being driven back south of the town by a strong KPA force. Walker needed no further proof that, in the absence of UN forces in defence in the coastal mountains, the North Koreans enjoyed unfettered freedom of movement.

On 10 August, the US Eighth Army commander formed Task Force P'ohang, comprising the ROKA 17th and 25th regiments, the ROKA 1st Anti-Guerrilla Battalion, the ROKA P'ohang Marine Battalion, and C Battery, US 18th FAB (75mm pack howitzers). The following day the ROKA 26th Regiment was activated at Taegu and immediately rushed east to join the task force at An'gang-ni. Only the ROKA 17th Regiment possessed any combat experience. Task Force P'ohang's brief was to clear the coastal mountains to the north of the An'gang-ni–P'ohang area of North Koreans.

However, by this time, and in what had now become synonymous with Walker's mobile defence tactics of the perimeter, Walker ordered Brigadier General Kim Suk

M116 75mm pack howitzers.

Wong's ROKA 3rd Division to dig in around the coastal town of Changsa-dong and seven miles south along the coastal road as a measure to block North Korean armour and artillery from reaching P'ohang 20 miles to the south.

In spite of the threatening nearness of the North Koreans, KMAG commander, Brigadier General Francis W. Farrell, responding to a question from Walker, stated that he would not need American troops to assist with the defence of P'ohang and the Yŏnil Airfield. Walker, however, was not convinced, and after a meeting with Emmerich at the airfield, decided to bolster his defences in the east. On 10 August, defining the urgency of the situation with immediate action, upon his return to his HQ at Taegu at 5.35 p.m., Walker dispatched orders by courier to the US 2nd Division commander at Kyŏngsang, Major General Lawrence B. Keiser: move the remainder of his 9th Regiment—the all African-American 3rd Battalion— to Yŏnil Airfield without delay. The battalion was reinforced with a company of engineers, a battery of field artillery, a battery of anti-aircraft self-propelled automatic weapons, a platoon of 4.2-inch mortars, and a company of tanks. Reporting directly to Walker, Keiser's second-in-command, Brigadier General Joseph S. Bradley, would be given command of the task, in what was known as Task Force Bradley. By midnight, Bradley assumed responsibility for the defence of Yŏnil.

The following day, 11 August, at 1 a.m. K Company and four vehicles of C Battery, 15th FAB, were ambushed just east of An'gang-ni. Springing the ambush, the North Koreans directed fire into the lead vehicle, killing the driver and causing his stalled truck to block the road. The enemy poured small-arms fire into the now stationary UN convoy as those who could escape fled back toward Kyongju.

Upon receiving a signal informing him of the ambush, Bradley ordered I Company down the road to An'gang-ni to rescue those caught in the ambush. However, the infantrymen were also ambushed to the west of P'ohang. Bradley reacted to the news by dispatching two 'Quad 50'- (four .50 calibre machine guns) mounted vehicles to the scene. However, elements of the KPA 766th IU that had set the ambush after having traversed the mountains from Yŏngdŏk, had gone to ground, leaving a scene of carnage in their wake. K Company had sustained 47 casualties, including seven dead. Twenty-five men of I Company failed to return to Yŏnil that afternoon, while C Battery, 15th FAB lost 25 in the ambush. Once more, in a desperate game of combat chess, Walker was forced to rethink his troop placements. That afternoon, he ordered Tank Company, 9th Infantry Regiment, US 2nd Division —equipped with M4A3E8 'Easy Eight' Sherman tanks—to move from Kyongju where they had been protecting repair work to a bridge, to Yŏnil Airfield. Turning to Task Force P'ohang. Walker issued simultaneous orders for ROKA 17th Regiment to leave An'gang-ni for the airfield.

With the unwanted reputation of having been the only American officer on the 38th Parallel when the North Koreans invaded the south on the morning of 25 June,

M114 203mm howitzer in action in Korea. (Photo US Army)

erstwhile KMAG assistant adviser to the ROKA 12th Regiment, Captain Joseph R. Darrigo, elected to ride in the first of five tanks that led the column to Yŏnil. Darrigo was fully aware that aerial reconnaissance had revealed that the North Koreans were still laying in ambush astride the main road. Air support, in the form of four F-51 Mustangs of the 40th Fighter-Interceptor Squadron (35th Group) stationed at Yŏnil Airfield, executed a strike on the North Korean position, forcing them to break cover. Caught in the open, many perished from tank .50 and .30 cal. Browning machine-gun fire. At 8.30 p.m. that night, the tanks became the first to arrive at Yŏnil Airfield, where they immediately assumed perimeter-defence positions.

On the morning of 11 August, Task Force P'ohang had only just left An'gang-ni when it came under heavy North Korean attack. The ROKA 25th Regiment lost two companies and the task force and ROKA Capital Division were forced back by overwhelming KPA firepower. Despite having four fighters shot down the previous day, F-51s tirelessly performed strafing missions out of Yŏnil Airfield. But by last light, KPA patrols were within three miles of the airfield. Over the ensuing two days, Walker ordered ROKA forces to retire to new positions. During the night, the fighter aircraft withdrew to a safe airfield, returning for daylight operations the next morning.

From high ground to the south and southwest, KPA artillery and mortars now opened fire, albeit ineffectively, on the airfield, creating concerns of an imminent attack. Amid reports of KPA troops entering P'ohang from 10 to 12 August, on 13 August FEAF made the decision to abandon the airfield. Without consulting the army, Fifth Air Force commander General Partridge endorsed Colonel Witty's decision to evacuate aircraft and groundcrew personnel. Both the 35th Fighter-Interceptor Group and the 6131st Fighter Wing—the latter by LSTs (landing ship tanks) on 15 August—returned to Tsuiki Air Base on Kyushu, Japan. The army units remained, however, and Yŏnil Airfield never came under effective KPA fire.

MacArthur and his chief of staff, the controversial Major General Edward Mallory 'Ned' Almond, were angered by FEAF's unilateral decision to evacuate Yŏnil Airfield. MacArthur passed on a message to FEAF command that he was not prepared to abandon the airfield and was desirous that the presence of crucial air support be maintained at the facility. However, all 51 F-51s were withdrawn.

On the coastal road, the ROKA 3rd Division faced inevitable defeat as their defence perimeter was squeezed ever south, pushing divisional HQ to Tŏksŏng-ni. Fire support for the beleaguered South Koreans came from the American cruiser USS *Helena* and three destroyers, and aircraft of the Fifth Air Force. All the while, LSTs were evacuating wounded soldiers, either to an anchored Korean hospital ship 500 yards offshore or directly to Pusan. Walker was left with no alternative option but to evacuate the South Koreans by sea so that they could live to fight another day.

South Korean police in the war-damaged P'ohang. (Photo US NARA)

NO MUNICH PEACE, BRITAIN TELLS RUSSIA

West 'Ready to Hear Genuine Proposals'

KOREA WRANGLE GOES ON

Britain and the U.S. told Russia in the Security Council yesterday that if she had any genuine proposals for peace in Korea, the West was ready and eager to hear them. Sir Gladwyn Jebb (Britain) said to Mr Malik with bitterness—"The very words 'peaceful settlement' in the mouth of the Soviet delegate are sufficient to cause anxiety." He recalled the "peaceful settlements" in Czechoslovakia in 1938 (Munich) and in 1948 (the Communist coup), and declared that Czechoslovakia had twice died in the name of peace.

'DETERMINED TO RESIST'

"This is not the kind of settlement fifty-two nations want in Korea. It is the kind we are determined to resist," he said. "The flagrant disregard of the will of the United Nations is the one thing that prevented, and still prevents, a peaceful settlement in Korea."

Mr Warren Austin, the chief U.S. delegate, said—"If there are any proposals to be made that will genuinely promote peace and security in the area conflict, the whole spirit of humanity demands that they be made without further delay."

He demanded that the Council give priority in its order of business to the resolution he had proposed, condemning North Korea for its defiance of U.N., and calling on all countries to help contain the Korean conflict by refusing to assist or encourage the North Korean authorities.

"The act of aggression against the Republic of Korea," Mr Austin went on, "is the most urgent business before U.N.

"If any delegate has proposals to make or resolutions to submit regarding the breach of the peace in Korea they can be made within the framework of the agenda item which has been before this Council for the last five weeks.

"The U.S. cannot agree that the question of Chinese representation can take precedence over the fact of armed aggression. Nor can the U.S. agree that the termination of aggression be made contingent on any other issue.

'MEN ARE DYING'

"So long as men are dying on the battlefield in defence of the United Nations, this Council will not wish to cheapen their suffering or sully their heroism by seeming to engage in the consideration of deals."

Mr Malik stuck to an agenda in which he proposed that Chinese representation should be considered first and the war in Korea second. He said that the U.S. resolution meant in plain language "the extension and the continuation the conflict."

The Council adjourned until to-day without taking any decision.

Aberdeen Press and Journal, Thursday, 3 August 1950

As darkness fell on 16 August, a flotilla of LSTs beached at Tŏksŏng-ni to extract 9,000 troops of the ROKA 3rd Divisions 22nd and 23rd regiments, 1,000 South Korean National Police, 1,000 divisional labourers and all the division's arms and equipment. Under sea and air escort, the South Koreans landed at Kuryongp'o-ri (Guryongpo-ri) on the eastern shore of the cape to the south of Yongil Bay. The next day, the force was deployed south of P'ohang and readied for battle.

Any KPA entry into P'ohang was transient—the principal objective lay farther to the south. Emboldened by the removal of the South Koreans in their way, the KPA 5th Division struck southward to the hills to the north of P'ohang. The KPA 12th Division now occupied hills to the west and southwest of the town, while the 2nd and 3rd battalions, KPA 2nd Regiment took up hilly positions closer to Yŏnil Airfield.

Following Walker's orders for the ROKA Capital Division to retire southward into a line on the ROKA 8th Division's right flank and ROKA I Corps to move its HQ to Yŏngch'ŏn, on 13 August the ROKA 17th Regiment, supported by tanks and artillery from Task Force Bradley, launched a counterattack on the hills to the north of P'ohang. Jumping off from An'gang-ni to the west, Task Force P'ohang marched on Kigye.

By 17 August, the North Koreans had been pushed back northward and the Taegu–P'ohang lateral corridor in the vicinity of An'gang-ni secured. The KPA 766th IU pulled back to mountains north of Kigye, while to the east, severely mauled by heavy American naval gunfire and air attacks, the whole KPA 12th Division was ordered to fall back at 8 p.m. The 2,400-feet Pihak-san peak six miles north of Kigye was selected as the assembly area for the division to regroup on 19 August. Here the 766th IU was dismantled and its troops absorbed by the KPA 12th Division's three infantry regiments. It was estimated, however, that the division could now only muster 5,000 men.

By 19 August, the ROKA Capital Division had advanced to just north of Kigye. The ROKA 3rd Division entered P'ohang and relieved Task Force Min, which was redeployed between the ROKA 1st and 6th divisions to the west in the ROKA II Corps sector.

Not displeased with the success of the early stages of the eastern counteroffensive, on 20 August Walker disbanded Task Force Bradley and retitled the unit at Yŏnil Airfield the 3rd Battalion, 9th Infantry Regiment, Reinforced. The US Eighth Army commander also dissolved Task Force P'ohang.

ROKA Army HQ claimed that, in the battle for P'ohang, the South Koreans had killed 3,800 KPA troops, in addition to capturing 181 enemy soldiers, 20 field guns, 33 mortars of various calibres, 160 machine guns, and 557 American M1 and 381 Japanese rifles.

By this time—26 August—morale among the UN forces along the P'ohang–Kigye front had improved dramatically, in the premature belief that the final threat to the Pusan Perimeter had been conclusively neutralized.

In the early hours of 27 August, a fresh assault by the KPA 12th Division in the ROKA Capital Division sector saw the 17th and 18th regiments falling back and the North Koreans retaking Kigye.

Crew and equipment of the 73rd Heavy Tank Battalion, US I Corps, await orders to board LSTs at Pusan. (Photo US Army)

At Taegu, a dismayed Walker met with his HQ staff. It took Walker only 30 minutes to reach a decision to address the latest development. Appointing the recently arrived Major General John B. Coulter as his deputy commander of the Eighth Army, Walker gave the Texan command of Task Force Jackson which he had established that morning. To be headquartered at Kyongju where the ROKA I Corps and KMAG senior staff also had their command centres, the task force would comprise ROKA I Corps, the 21st Regiment, US 24th Division, the 3rd Battalion, 9th Regiment, US 2nd Division, and the 73rd Tank Battalion (less C Company), the latter equipped with M26 Pershing tanks. Coulter was tasked with immediately reversing the latest KPA gains and establishing a fresh line that ran ten miles north of Kigye to 12 miles north of P'ohang.

However, Coulter's planned attack for 28 August failed to materialize due to ROKA I Corps and ROKA 3rd Division in P'ohang contending that overwhelming enemy numbers, high casualty levels and troop exhaustion prevented them from complying with Coulter's orders to launch the attack. ROKA 3rd Division commander,

Brigadier General Kim Suk Won, not only refused to attack, but informed KMAG adviser Emmerich that he was going to withdraw his command post from P'ohang. When Emmerich was emphatic that he was not leaving, the South Korean became overwrought with unbridled anxiety as he knew that to leave now in the face of the enemy would bring dishonour.

At Eighth Army HQ, Walker, having pinned his hopes on Task Force Jackson stemming the latest North Korean offensive, issued a statement to the ROK Army: "It is my belief, that the over-extended enemy is making his last gasp, while United Nations forces are daily becoming stronger and stronger. The time has now come for everyone to stand in place and fight, or advance to a position which will give us greater tactical advantage from which the counter-offensive can be launched. If our present positions are pierced, we must counterattack at once, destroy the enemy and restore the positions ... To you officers and soldiers of the Army of the Republic of Korea, I ask that you rise as one and stop the enemy on your front in his tracks."

The South Koreans paid lip service to Walker's appeal. Over the next few days, every time American-supported ground gains were made then left to the South Koreans to hold, they failed to do so when the KPA counterattacked. An exasperated Walker ordered Lieutenant Colonel Stephen's US 21st Infantry to assume control of the strategic tract of ground to the immediate north and northwest of P'ohang from the ROKA 3rd Division.

On 29 and 30 August, naval vessels in the Sea of Japan, in support of the faltering ROKA 3rd Division, continued to pound KPA 5th Division positions at Hunghae, five miles north of P'ohang. However, aerial reconnaissance conducted on 1 September revealed KPA troops concentrations assembling in the mountains north of the Kigye–P'ohang line.

At mid-point between P'ohang and Hunghae, bloody, protracted fighting took place on Hill 99 as UN forces repeatedly tried to dislodge well-entrenched elements of the KPA 5th Division from the commanding position. Despite air, artillery and naval gunfire support, the ROKA 3rd Division's 23rd Regiment suffered very heavy casualties in its attempts to take the hill.

The next day, K Company, US 21st Regiment was equally unsuccessful in taking Hill 99 in the face of obstinate North Korean resistance. By late afternoon, the company could only muster 25 of its men.

At around 1.30 a.m. on 3 September, elements of the KPA 12th Division penetrated the ROKA Capital Division sector, pushing the 17th and 18th regiments from hills 334, 438 and 445 to the south and southwest of Kigye. By first light, the North Koreans straddled the Taegu–P'ohang corridor just to the east of An'gang-ni. The Capital Division was on the brink of disintegrating.

A US M26 Pershing tank in hull-down position to optimize gun elevation. (Photo US Marine Corps)

The UN forces had to plug the serious breach, compelling Coulter to move the 2nd Battalion, 21st Regiment (2/21st), to the outskirts of Kyongju, where battalion commander Lieutenant Colonel Gines Perez placed his troops in defensive positions along three sides of the town, including on high ground to the east that commanded the Kyongju–P'ohang road. At the same time, Walker rushed the newly activated ROKA 7th Division into the sector, where the division's 5th Regiment reached Yŏngch'ŏn that afternoon. A few hours later, the 3rd Regiment (less the 1st Battalion) arrived at Kyongju. From the Yŏnil Airfield defences, Walker granted Coulter permission to utilize the 3rd Battalion, 8th Regiment, the 9th Regimental Tank Company and the 15th FAB as he deemed necessary. Only in a dire emergency should D and A batteries of the 865th and 933rd anti-aircraft battalions be taken from the airfield.

During the night of 3/4 September, the ROKA I Corps front crumbled, resulting in total pandemonium within the South Korean ranks. North Korean tanks obliterated an ROKA artillery battery before causing two battalions of the ROKA 5th Regiment to bombshell in disarray. Shortly after 2 a.m., the KPA forces entered An'gang-ni, and an hour later, the ROKA Capital Division evacuated its HQ from the town.

By midday, the North Koreans had blocked the An'gang-ni–Kyongju road three miles north of Kyongju. With the collapse of the ROKA I Corps, Coulter was suddenly faced with yawning gaps in the front created by the precipitate departure of the South Koreans southward. To the southwest of An'gang-ni and northwest of Kyongju, an eight-mile gap had opened up between the ROKA Capital and 8th divisions in the mountainous area west of the Hyongsan valley. Appreciating the threat that this weak point posed to the Kyongju–Pusan corridor, Coulter moved the 21st Regiment into the broad valley to block any enemy advances on Kyongju. Positioning four tanks around his command post in the town, Coulter was determined not to add Kyongju to the UN's latest litany of losses.

To the east, the situation was as critical. At 5.30 a.m. on 5 September, news was received that the ROKA 22nd Regiment had vacated P'ohang as American tanks in the town came under direct fire from heavy machine-gun and self-propelled-gun fire.

A ROKA diversionary landing north of P'ohang on 15 September. (Photo US NARA)

UN airstrikes and artillery silenced the North Koreans, but Emmerich still felt it expedient to remove all equipment, combat matériel and supplies from the Yŏnil Airfield.

Shortly after midnight on 6 September, the ROKA 3rd Division wilted under enemy artillery and mortar fire, and amid reports that the division's commander and his two deputies had mysteriously—and conveniently—fallen ill, the South Koreans deserted P'ohang once more. ROKA immediately replaced the respective I Corps and 3rd Division commanders.

Walker continued to commit manpower into the area in a bid to prevent imminent capitulation of ROKA forces to his east. While underway to relieve the Marines on the lower Naktong River on 4 September, Major General John H. Church, commander of the US 24th Division since the capture by KPA forces of the previous incumbent, Major General William F. Dean, received fresh orders to move his division to Kyongju instead. By 7 a.m. on 6 September, the whole division had arrived at Kyongju. Task Force Jackson was now redesignated Task Force Church as the general assumed command of all operations in the east. Coulter returned to Taegu to recommence his planning duties. Church's first priority was to shift his command post four miles southward to the less vulnerable and congested Choyang-ni.

In torrential monsoon downpours from 8 to 10 September, bitter fighting raged between the UN forces and the North Koreans for control of the An'gang-ni–Kyongju corridor and the commanding hills 285 and 300 on the western fringes of the corridor. To the southwest of Yŏnil Airfield, an estimated 1,600-strong KPA force closed on hills 482 and 510 held by elements of the ROKA 3rd Division.

Late on 9 September, Church raised Task Force Davidson to restore the Yŏnil Airfield's defences, previously stripped to augment much-needed manpower elsewhere. Commanded by combat engineer and assistant commander of the US 24th Division, Major General Garrison H. Davidson, the eponymous task force comprised the 19th Regiment (less the 3rd Battalion, US 24th Division), the 3rd Battalion, 9th Regiment (US 2nd Division), the 13th FAB (105mm howitzers, US 24th Division), C Battery, 15th FAB (105mm howitzers, US 2nd Division), A Company, 3rd Engineer Combat Battalion (US 24th Division), the 9th Regimental Tank Company, two batteries of anti-aircraft automatic guns, and a miscellany of support units.

Early in the morning of 10 September, Davidson flew from Kyongju to his task force's designated assembly area at Yŏngdŏk-tong, a mile to the south of the airfield. Colonel Emmerich, who was waiting for Davidson's light aircraft as it landed on a road, briefed the task force commander about a strong North Korean presence on Hill 131 to the south of the two ROKA regiments—23rd and 26th—on perimeter defence duty at the airfield.

After carefully assessing the North Korean threat to Yŏnil, the two officers agreed that Hill 131 would have to be retaken during the hours of darkness to allow the task

A US Fifth Air Force B-26 Invader drops its payload over Korea. (Photo US NARA)

force easier passage through the ROKA 3rd Division to capture Hill 482. The South Korean commander was duly informed of the plan, and the fact that the taking of Hill 131 was his responsibility.

That night, elements of the ROKA 3rd Division, assisted by the ROKA 3rd Engineer Battalion in a combat role and under the competent leadership of KMAG adviser, Captain Walter J. Hutchins, successfully reclaimed Hill 131.

At first light on 11 September, the 1st Battalion, US 19th Regiment (1/19th), spearheaded an attack south and west of the now secure Hill 131 toward Hill 482. By 9.30 a.m., the 1/19th had taken the first high ground two miles west from the task force's point of departure without firing a shot. The 2/19th now passed through the 1/19th for the main assault on Hill 482, only a mile farther west. However, for the remainder of the day, the 2/19th had to dig in as KPA machine-gun fire checked their advance up the hill. In the morning, Australian aircraft hit the KPA hilltop positions with napalm, followed on the ground by a preparatory artillery bombardment. By lunchtime, the 2/19th had fought their way to the top of the hill, capturing it from the North Koreans. A few hours later, ROKA forces relieved the Americans on Hill 482. In concurrent action, ROKA 3rd Division troops finally captured Hill 300 to the south of An'gang-ni after several days of costly fighting.

The crew of
an M24 tank
of the 24th
Reconnaissance,
24th Division
along the Naktong
River front in
a posed shot.
(Sgt Riley/ DoD)

Taking stock on 12 September, US Eighth Army HQ concluded that the North Korean offensive along the eastern corridors had been successfully repelled. The battered remnants of the KPA 5th and 12th divisions were in full retreat northward, tailed by the ROKA 3rd and Capital divisions respectively as they withdrew.

On 15 September, Walker disbanded Task Force Church and returned command of the ROKA I Corps to the South Koreans. The US 24th Division was ordered back to a regrouping of UN forces south of Taegu. The 9th Regiment, US 2nd Division, would remain as Eighth Army reserve at Kyongju. It was accepted that ROKA forces did most of the fighting on the ground, but with the support of American armour, artillery, elements of infantry and the hardy KMAG advisers. The fact that the UN forces enjoyed unchallenged control of air and naval firepower was a major contributing factor to its successes in the east. Finally, the North Koreans were critically hamstrung, and tellingly so, by insufficient and incompetent logistics and communications support.

5. THE TIDE TURNS

Following successive defeats throughout July 1950 at the hands of the North Korean People's Army's blitzkrieg-style juggernaut, on 29 July US Eighth Army commander, Lieutenant General Walton H. Walker, had made his punchy and emphatic 'stand or die' order to his troops. Walker's mission would be to hold a defensive line—the Pusan Perimeter—to buy time for the American-led United Nations forces to arrive at the southern tip of the Korean peninsula in sufficient strengths to facilitate a massed counteroffensive to drive the North Koreans back north of the 38th Parallel.

It had been a tall order, especially in the early stages when Walker's 'army' only consisted of two understrength divisions, the US 24th and 25th, and the 1st Cavalry Division. In due course during the crisis, reinforcements had arrived in the form of the newly raised 1st Marine Provisional Brigade, the 5th RCT, regiments of the US 2nd Division and, in the latter stages, the UK 27th Infantry Brigade. All of the general's requirements would land at the natural harbour in Pusan, where docking facilities for up to 30 sea vessels could handle 45,000 tons a day. By the middle of August more than 500 American medium tanks had been discharged at the port.

Through the latter half of July and most of August, successive North Korean divisional attacks had infiltrated and sorely tested Walker's defence line, from Masan in the south to Taegu in the north to P'ohang on the east coast. In a second round of attacks commencing on 27 August, Walker faced a more orchestrated enemy simultaneously penetrating five points on his perimeter. In the first fortnight in September, the Americans would sustain their greatest number of casualties of the war.

All the while, Walker skilfully and uniquely had utilized his limited resources by employing mobile combat tactics in rushing reserves to where his defence line came under the greatest threat at any one point in time. In partnership with indispensable naval and air support, without which the US Eighth Army would most likely have been overrun, Walker held out long enough to see his now flagging endurance finally stall the North Koreans offensive around 12 September. The tide began to turn in the United Nations Command's favour.

By 27 September, with the US I and X corps firmly in control, the remains of the pulverized KPA corps, numbering 20–30,000, limped home to the north. At the beginning of the month, along the Pusan Perimeter the 13 KPA infantry divisions, one armoured division, two armoured brigades and one security brigade had numbered 98,000 men.

Fresh American reinforcements await in-country deployment. (Photo US Defense Department)

For Walker, it was also a costly campaign. From 5 July to 16 September the US Eighth Army casualties comprised 4,280 killed in action, 12,377 wounded, 2107 missing and 401 taken prisoner.

Arguably, the US Far East Air Force (FEAF) made the biggest impact on the outcome of any phase of the Korean War in August 1950. By this time, the Fifth Air Force had placed tactical air control parties (TACPs) with each American and South Korean divisional, regimental and corps HQs. American fighter aircraft, flying from bases in Japan, would report in to the tactical air control centre at the rate of two every 15 minutes to receive mission information and be directed to the relevant TACP. By 23 August, 29 North American T-6 Texan 'Mosquitoes' of the 6147th Tactical Air Control Group were providing dawn-to-dusk airborne tactical coordination. In August, FEAF flew 7,400 ground support sorties, up from 4,600 the previous month.

During August, while enjoying air supremacy, FEAF conducted a strategic programme of interdiction bombing raids against specific war-related enemy targets north of the 38th Parallel, hitting military installations, bridges, rail marshalling yards, harbours and factories. The B-26 Marauder and B-29 Superfortress increasingly disrupted the North Koreans' already fragile logistics chain to their troops besieging the Pusan Perimeter.

North American T-6 Texan 'Mosquito' in Korean revetments. (Photo US Air Force)

On the ground, the consistency and reliability of the UN forces logistics network completely overshadowed that of the North Koreans. Perfected after the D-Day invasion during the Second World War, the 'Red Ball Express' supply chain assured Walker of anything available from Japan in a very short space of time, critical during the major KPA offensive in late August. By the end of July the system had developed into the epitome of efficiency. Every night at 11.30 p.m., an express train would freight supplies to Sasebo, arriving at the American naval base in Japan at 5.42 a.m. the following morning. Having loaded cargo directly from the train, a ship would sail for Pusan daily at 1.30 p.m. Arriving in Korea at 4 a.m. the next morning, Red Ball Express trucks were ready to rush supplies to various points at the front. From mid-August, daily flights by C-119 Boxcars from Tachikawa air base in Japan directly into Taegu heralded the discontinuation of the Red Ball Express, except for secondary distribution from Taegu.

Back in the United States, the 6th (M46 Pattons), the 70th (M26 Pershings and M4A3 Shermans) and the 73rd ((M26 Pershings) tank battalions had been mobilized and combat trained. Departing San Francisco on 23 July, the armour arrived in Pusan on 7 August. This was followed on 28 July when the 15,200-ton SS *Luxembourg Victory* sailed from San Francisco with 80 medium tanks in its holds. On 16 August, equipped with M26 Pershings, the 2nd Division's 72nd Medium Tank Battalion docked at Pusan.

In the same month, the US 3rd Infantry Division, commanded by Major General Robert H. Soule, was moved to Korea. On 19 August, MacArthur submitted a request to the Department of the Army for military personnel, including troops, to activate US I and X corps. By 6 September, 229 officers and 2,200 men from US Eighth Army rear echelons in Japan had been posted to Korea. This was in addition to the more than 11,000 officers and other ranks that had been moved across from Japan during August.

As at 1 September, including the US Fifth Air Force, the UK 27th Infantry Brigade and ROKA forces, the UNC's strength stood at 180,000 men. This number was complemented by a further 33,650 FEAF personnel, including 330 of the Royal Australian Air Force.

On 20 August, the British government announced that it would dispatch two regular infantry battalions from Hong Kong to Korea. Nine days later, UK 27th Infantry Brigade commanded by Brigadier Basil Coad and comprising the 1st Battalion, Middlesex Regiment and 1st Battalion, Argyll and Sutherland Highlanders, arrived at Pusan from Hong Kong. That night they were railed to Kyŏngsang, ten miles southeast of Taegu.

Eventually, combat elements from 15 member countries of the United Nations would fight alongside the Americans and South Koreans in the war against the north. When, on 29 June 1950, the Royal Navy pledged its services to the conflict, Australia

F-51D Mustangs of 77 Squadron, Royal Australian Air Force, Iwakuni, Japan, 1950. (Photo US Air Force)

placed the destroyer HMAS *Bataan* and the frigate HMAS *Shoalhaven* at MacArthur's disposal. Prime Minister Robert Menzies had also committed the fully operational 77th Mustang Fighter Squadron, Royal Australian Air Force (RAAF) to Korean operations from its British Commonwealth Occupation Force base at Iwakuni in Japan. Commanded by Wing Commander Lou Spence, the squadron conducted its first combat sortie from Iwakuni on 2 July. In August, 40 pilots from the 77th flew 800 sorties, amounting to 1,745 flying hours. In July and August, they accounted for 35 North Korean T-34 tanks and 226 military vehicles.

As early as the first week in July 1950, UNC commander General Douglas MacArthur was already discussing the idea of an amphibious-based offensive with his chief of staff, General Almond. It would be to the rear of KPA positions and within striking distance of Seoul. With the 1st Cavalry Division spearheading the invasion, Operation Bluehearts was set for 22 July. But the failure of American and South Korean forces to halt the KPA's relentless march southward left MacArthur with no option but to scupper the plan on 10 July.

However, in Tokyo, Far East Command staff continued to look at plans for an invasion. On 23 July, senior staff were circulated with the framework of Operation Chromite, suggesting three possible sites for an amphibious landing. Situated on the west coast, Inch'ŏn, the second largest port in Korea, was selected for an invasion in September. At the time, though, the tenuous situation along the Pusan Perimeter precluded the increasingly frustrated MacArthur from going firm on his plans, as reflected in a 29 July signal: "In Korea the hopes that I had entertained to hold out the 1st Marine Division [Brigade] and the 2d Infantry Division for the enveloping counter blow have not been fulfilled and it will be necessary to commit these units to Korea on the south line rather than ... their subsequent commitment along a separate axis in mid-September. I now plan to commit my sole reserve in Japan, the 7th Infantry Division, as soon as it can be brought to an approximate combat strength."

As the North Koreans fell on Walker's forces in the second major offensive in late August, MacArthur appointed the 58-year-old General Almond as commander of the newly activated X Corps for the planned invasion. The backbone of the US X Corps, the 1st Marine and 7th Infantry divisions started to assemble in Japan. At a top-flight meeting with senior naval and army personnel in Tokyo on 20 July, MacArthur made it very clear that they had to wrest the initiative away from the North Koreans. While the enemy threw everything they had at Walker, they had become blasé about protecting their rear. It would make sound tactical sense to trap the North Koreans from the north.

Brigadier General Courtney Whitney, General Douglas MacArthur and Major General Edward Almond observe the preparatory shelling of Inch'ŏn from the USS *Mount McKinley*, 15 September 1950.

On 6 September, MacArthur messaged his senior commanders informing them that 15 September 1950 would be D-Day for the first major counteroffensive of the war: the UN forces invasion at Inch'ŏn.

MacArthur faced off protestations from some of his commanders. The UN allies' fortunes were starting to turn as the tenacious Walker gained the upper hand over an ever-weakening North Korean threat to the Pusan line of defence—the Red tide was finally ebbing. On 8 September MacArthur sent a final message to Washington. The time for debating was over and the UN Inch'ŏn invasion would happen on 15 September:

There is no question in my mind as to the feasibility of the operation and I regard its chance of success as excellent. I go further and believe that it represents the only hope of wresting the initiative from the enemy and thereby presenting an opportunity for a decisive blow. To do otherwise is to commit us to a war of indefinite duration, of gradual attrition, and of doubtful results.

There is no slightest possibility ... of our force being ejected from the Pusan beachhead. The envelopment from the north will instantly relieve the pressure on the south perimeter and, indeed, is the only way that this can be accomplished. The success of the enveloping movement from the north does not depend upon the rapid juncture of the X Corps and the Eighth Army. The seizure of the heart of the enemy distributing system in the Seoul area will completely dislocate the logistical supply of his forces now operating in South Korea and therefore will ultimately result in their disintegration. This, indeed, is the primary purpose of the movement. Caught between our northern and southern forces, both of which are completely self-sustaining because of our absolute air and naval supremacy, the enemy cannot fail to be ultimately shattered through disruption of his logistical support and our combined combat activities.

For the reasons stated, there are no material changes under contemplation in the operation as planned and reported to you. The embarkation of the troops and the preliminary air and naval preparations are proceeding according to schedule.

Index

Acknowledgements & Sources

As always, my heart felt gratitude to my dear friend Colonel Dudley Wall for all the hard work and dedication that is synonymous with his outstanding drawings of maps and the machines of war, and images from his vast, personal collection of militaria. Special thanks to Chris Cocks, who remains so much more than just a commissioning editor. The following were consulted:

Appleman, Roy E., 'South to the Naktong, North to the Yalu (June–November 1950)', *United States in the Korean War*, Center of Military History, United States Army, Washington, D.C., 1992

Central Intelligence Agency documents (declassified)

Fehrenbach, T. R., *This Kind of War: The Classic Korean War History*, Potomac Books, 2000

Gugeler, Russell A., *Combat Actions in Korea*, Center of Military History, United States Army, Washington D.C., 1954

Hastings, Max, *The Korean War*, Pan, London, 1987

Korean War Project, www.koreanwar.org/

Sloan, Bill, *The Darkest Summer; Pusan and Inch'ŏn 1950*, Simon & Schuster Paperbacks, New York, 2009

Tucker, Spencer C. (Ed.), *Encyclopedia of the Korean War*, Checkmark Books, New York, 2002).

United States Army Records, National Archives & Records Administration, College Park, Maryland, USA

About the Author

Born in Southern Rhodesia, now Zimbabwe, historian and author Gerry van Tonder came to Britain in 1999. Specializing in military history, Gerry started his writing career with titles about twentieth-century guerrilla and open warfare in southern Africa, including the co-authored definitive *Rhodesia Regiment 1899–1981*. Gerry presented a copy of this title to the regiment's former colonel-in-chief, Her Majesty the Queen. Having written over twenty books, Gerry writes extensively for several Pen & Sword military history series including 'Cold War 1945–1991', 'Military Legacy' (focusing on the heritage of British cities), 'Echoes of the Blitz', and 'History of Terror'.

Other Titles by the Author

SS Einsatzgruppen: Nazi Death Squads 1939–1945
Irgun: Revisionist Zionism 1931–1948
Sino-Indian War: October–November 1962
Echoes of the Coventry Blitz
Red China: Mao Crushes Chiang's Kuomintang, 1949
North Korea Invades the South: Across the 38th Parallel, June 1950
Berlin Blockade: Soviet Chokehold and the Great Allied Airlift 1948–1949
Malayan Emergency: Triumph of the Running Dogs 1948–1960
Nottingham's Military Legacy
Sheffield's Military Legacy
Derby in 50 Buildings
Chesterfield's Military Heritage
Mansfield Through Time
Rhodesian African Rifles/Rhodesia Native Regiment Book of Remembrance
Lt-Gen Keith Coster: A Life in Uniform
Rhodesian Combined Forces Roll of Honour 1966-1981
Rhodesia Regiment 1899–1981
Operation Lighthouse: Intaf in the Rhodesian Bush War 1972–1980 (2019)
North of the Red Line: Recollections of the Border War by Members of the South African Armed Forces: 1966–1989

Other Pen & Sword titles by Gerry van Tonder

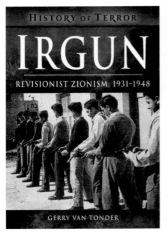

HISTORY OF TERROR

IRGUN
REVISIONIST ZIONISM, 1931–1948

GERRY VAN TONDER

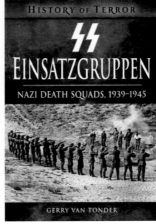

HISTORY OF TERROR

SS EINSATZGRUPPEN
NAZI DEATH SQUADS, 1939–1945

GERRY VAN TONDER

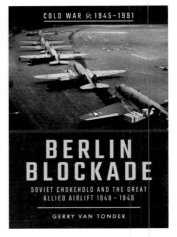

COLD WAR 1945–1991

BERLIN BLOCKADE
SOVIET CHOKEHOLD AND THE GREAT ALLIED AIRLIFT 1948–1949

GERRY VAN TONDER

COLD WAR 1945–1991

MALAYAN EMERGENCY
TRIUMPH OF THE RUNNING DOGS 1948–1960

GERRY VAN TONDER

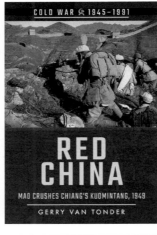

COLD WAR 1945–1991

RED CHINA
MAO CRUSHES CHIANG'S KUOMINTANG, 1949

GERRY VAN TONDER

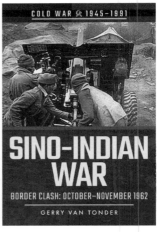

COLD WAR 1945–1991

SINO-INDIAN WAR
BORDER CLASH: OCTOBER–NOVEMBER 1962

GERRY VAN TONDER

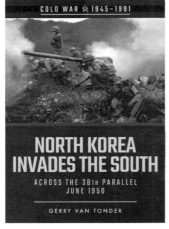

COLD WAR 1945–1991

NORTH KOREA INVADES THE SOUTH
ACROSS THE 38TH PARALLEL JUNE 1950

GERRY VAN TONDER

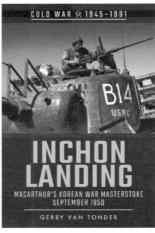

COLD WAR 1945–1991

INCHON LANDING
MACARTHUR'S KOREAN WAR MASTERSTOKE SEPTEMBER 1950

GERRY VAN TONDER

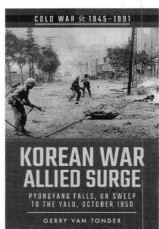

COLD WAR 1945–1991

KOREAN WAR ALLIED SURGE
PYONGYANG FALLS, UN SWEEP TO THE YALU, OCTOBER 1950

GERRY VAN TONDER